FAITH AS POLITICS

Reflections in Commemoration of Beyers Naudé (1915-2004)

Edited by Henning Melber

THE NORDIC AFRICA INSTITUTE
UPPSALA 2015

INDEXING TERMS:

Naudé, Beyers (1915-2004)
Anti-apartheid activists
Political history
Apartheid
Race relations
Religion
Church
Christianity
Clergy
Theology
Reconciliation
South Africa

The opinions expressed in this volume are those of the authors
and do not necessarily reflect the views of the Nordic Africa Institute.

ISBN 978-91-7106-780-7
© 2015 The authors and The Nordic Africa Institute
Cover photo: Collage
Layout: Henrik Alfredsson, The Nordic Africa Institute
Print on demand: Lightning Source UK Ltd

For their generous support in contributing with photos to this book, the authors wish to express their gratitude to Jim Elfström, Lars Herneklint, Fredrik Wassermeyer, AMP Film, Raymond Perrier, the Denis Hurley Center, the World Council of Churches and the United Nations Photo Library.

Contents

Preface 5

Faith as Politics – and Politics as Faith: Beyers Naudé and Dag Hammarskjöld
Henning Melber 7

Ecumenical Witness for Social Justice: Beyers Naudé and Denis Hurley
N. Barney Pityana 19

Beyers Naudé as Teacher: Memories of a Student
Ben Khumalo-Seegelken 37

A Response to Ben Khumalo-Seegelken
Hans S.A. Engdahl 42

Beyers Naudé's Prophetic Voice
Horst Kleinschmidt 45

A Response to Horst Kleinschmidt
Birgitta Karlström-Dorph 51

Beyers Naudé and the Theology of Reconciliation
Christo Lombard 55

A Response to Christo Lombard
Rune Forsbeck 73

UkuBuyisana
Ben Khumalo-Seegelken 79

Contributors 80

Preface

It was in May 2014 when Hans Engdahl observed in a conversation that a year later would mark the 100th birthday of *Oom Bey*, as the Reverend Beyers Naudé was fondly known.[1] He was a role model not only for those committed Afrikaans-speaking white South Africans who, in their fight to achieve a home for all South Africans in a democratic society, were willing to speak truth to power. In being made aware of this centenary, an earlier concerted effort came to mind: in December 2011 two symposia were held in Uppsala and Oslo respectively in a collaboration between the Dag Hammarskjöld Foundation, the Nordic Africa Institute, the Dag Hammarskjöld programme at Voksenåsen and the Luthuli Museum. These symposia commemorated two Nobel Peace Laureates, Dag Hammarskjöld and Albert Luthuli, half a century after they were awarded the prize.[2]

An idea floated by Hans Engdahl was turned into a proposal and resonated with Iina Soiri at the Nordic Africa Institute. The Institute now teamed up with Bernt Jonsson at the Mission Church in Uppsala (Uppsala Missionskyrka) and the Church of Sweden (Svenska kyrkan) to explore a similar recognition of the legacy of another remarkable person, Beyers Naudé, and commemorate his contribution to the democratic transition in South Africa. Thanks to funding provided by the Nordic Africa Institute and the material and practical support of the other institutions, a small team representing all the partners was able to plan and organise accordingly. On 10 May 2015 a service in the Missionskyrkan was held in memory of Oom Bey. The next day, a symposium on "Faith as Politics – South African Perspectives" took place at the same venue. This publication is a compilation of the presentations at that event. In addition, the lecture given by Barney Pityana on 10 May 2015 at the Denis Hurley Centre in Durban is included, as is an introductory essay.

This modest collection is a tribute to a great person. It recalls the virtues and principles of Oom Bey and his contribution to social and political change in South Africa. At the same time, the following reflections are also small tokens of gratitude for the existence of people such as Oom Bey. They serve as lodestars in our humble efforts to contribute to a better world. They give us strength and confidence. They reaffirm our conviction that it is not us who are wrong, but the inequalities and injustices we are confronted with. And they remind us that we have to do something about them.

Henning Melber
Uppsala, August 2015

---

[1] *Oom* is the Afrikaans word for uncle and is widely used locally to address elderly people with respect but also a degree of familiarity and identification.

[2] The contributions to the events were published as Tor Sellström (ed.), *Albert Luthuli and Dag Hammarskjöld – Leaders and Visionaries*. Uppsala: Dag Hammarskjöld Foundation and Nordic Africa Institute 2012. Accessible at www.shar.es/15raPb.

> As Christian church, the church must be an advocate for the poor, the oppressed, the hungry, the voiceless, the unjustly treated – notwithstanding whether they are white or black.
>
> Beyers Naudé [1]

> Hunger is my native place in the land of the passions. Hunger for fellowship, hunger for righteousness – for a fellowship founded on righteousness, and a righteousness attained in fellowship.
>
> Dag Hammarskjöld [2]

---

[1] From "Die profetiese roeping van die kerk in hierdie tyd," deposited in the Beyers Naudé Archive in Stellenbosch. Quoted in English translation by Robert Vosloo in an unpublished paper, "The Dutch Reformed Church, Beyers Naudé and the ghost of Cottesloe," presented at the annual meeting of the Church Historical Society of Southern Africa (CHSSA) in Potchefstroom, 16-18 August 2010, p. 8. Accessible at www.bit.ly/1XJRJNH.

[2] An entry from 1950 in the private notebook he left behind, which was posthumously published (Hammarskjöld 1983: 43).

Faith as Politics – and Politics as Faith: Beyers Naudé and Dag Hammarskjöld

Henning Melber

> What is faith, understood not as consoling belief, but as robust agent for the good in the face even of terrible difficulties? (Lipsey 2013: 453)

This essay traces and presents the commonalities in the practised lives of Dag Hammarskjöld and Beyers Naudé, two firm believers in humanity whose actions spoke as loudly as their words. They never met, but after engaging with their visions and convictions, it seems not too far-fetched to me to assume that they could have been soulmates. The Secretary-General of the United Nations visited South Africa only once, in early 1961, in an effort to resolve the impasse over the racist domestic policy of the apartheid regime. He was not very successful (cf. Sellström 2011; Saunders 2011).

Another planned visit had to be postponed because of the crisis in the Congo. His death in September 1961, when his plane crashed upon approaching the North Rhodesian mining town of Ndola on his way to meet Moise Tshombé to seek a solution to the Katanga secession (Melber 2014), meant that he never returned to South Africa. Maybe at a later time Hammarskjöld and Naudé might have met – in South Africa, in Uppsala or elsewhere. I am convinced they would have been able to recognise with ease their many common values and shared beliefs. These were essentials were so obviously similar, not only in terms of morality, but also in their translation of morality into practice.

The Uppsala Tradition

Beyers Naudé was no stranger to Uppsala. As he stated in an interview in 1995: "I was constantly visiting Uppsala and I also attended the World Council Conference there in 1968" (Sellström 1999: 182). The mid-Swedish city has a long ecumenical tradition and has been home to several Nobel Peace Laureates: Bishop Nathan Söderblom (1930), Dag Hammarskjöld (posthumously 1961) and Alva Myrdal (1982). Dag Hammarskjöld, the second Secretary-General of the United Nations, in a speech even made reference to the "Uppsala Tradition", which he summarised as "a spiritual legacy beyond ... boundaries" (Hammarskjöld 1956c: 164). In terms of his characterisation of the disciples of the Uppsala Tradition, it becomes obvious that he was indeed referring to an approach and mind-set of a particular "species" beyond boundaries. His definition is fully applicable to people like Beyers Naudé:

> At their best the representatives of this legacy show the quiet self-assurance of people firmly rooted in their own world, but they are, at the same time and for that very reason, able to accept and develop a true world citizenship. At the best they are not afraid to like the man in their enemy and they know that such liking gives an insight which is a source of strength. They have learned patience in dealings with mightier powers. They know that their only hope is that justice will prevail and for that reason they like to speak for justice. However, they also know the dangers and temptations of somebody speaking for justice without humility. They have learned that they can stand strong only if faithful to their own ideals, and they have shown the courage to follow the guidance of those ideals to ends which sometimes, temporarily, have been very bitter. And finally, the spirit is one of peace… (Hammarskjöld 1956c: 164f.)

Understood this way, the Uppsala Tradition is one of global human engagement. It is represented at its best by Beyers Naudé as much as by Dag Hammarskjöld. As the editors of a compilation of 40 oral testimonies by those close to Beyers Naudé note in their introduction, he was "a crosser of borders" with "a pronounced ability to subvert the barriers of identity construed by culture, race and religion, coupled with the ability to adjust the context of his theological convictions accordingly" (Coetzee/Muller/Hansen 2015: x).

Universal Faith

This notion resonates with the perspectives and practices of the global citizen Hammarskjöld, whose spirituality was not limited to a certain theological or teleological mind-set, but was an all-embracing approach towards humanity and human interaction in a spirit of mutual respect and recognition of what in today's jargon would be termed "otherness." As "priest of a secular church" (Bouman 2005: 41), he considered the United Nations as "an instrument of faith" (Hammarskjöld 1954: 352). In one of his rare extemporaneous speeches, prompted by a moving encounter during a cultural event performed in his honour, Hammarskjöld addressed the Indian Council of World Affairs by stressing the universality of human dimensions: "With respect to the United Nations as a symbol of faith, it may … be said that to every man it stands as a kind of 'yes' to the ability of man to form his own destiny, and form his own destiny so as to create a world where dignity of man can come fully into its own." (Hammarskjöld 1956a: 660).

Hammarskjöld conceived and created a "Room of Quiet", opened in 1957, as a United Nations Mediation Room on the ground floor of the organisation's headquarters. As he explained in a leaflet for visitors, it was designed as "a place where the doors may be open to the infinite lands of thought and prayer". Given its universal character, "none of the symbols to which we are accustomed in our meditation could be used". Instead, "simple things which speak to us all with the same language" were selected. A solid block of iron ore was the centrepiece, understood by Hammarskjöld as "a reminder of that cornerstone of endurance and faith on which all human endeavor must be based". [3]

What Hammarskjöld noted in his then unknown intimate notebook in the same year, when he publicly contemplated the Uppsala Tradition, might well also have been an entry into a notebook by Beyers Naudé: "Beyond obedience, its attention fixed on the goal – freedom from fear. Beyond fear – openness to life. And beyond that – love" (Hammarskjöld 1983: 110). Oom Bey is quoted as follows:

The Meditation Room at the UN Headquarters, enlarged and remodeled upon Hammarskjöld's initiative in 1957. The fresco in the background is the work of Swedish artist Bo Beskow.

> You can never be fully human unless you've discovered the humanity in other human beings. Don't close your eyes to the injustices of your own country by trying to solve the injustices of another country. That's an evasion of Christian responsibility.[4]

And again Dag Hammarskjöld in 1956:

> The "great" commitment all too easily obscures the "little" one. But without the humility and warmth which you have to develop in your relations to the few with whom you are personally involved, you will never be able to do anything for the many. (Hammarskjöld 1983: 113)

According to Gisela Albrecht (2004: 98), Beyers Naudé never considered his pilgrimage as a primarily political journey, but always as one determined by faith. He was guided by what he understood as obedience to God. This was an obedience that made him ultimately (and far too late, as he often said) realise what is right and what is wrong. This insight and its consequences forced him into confrontation with all that had mattered to him before then, with everything he had been taught was holy since his birth: his church, the state and especially his own Afrikaner people. Instead, his faith translated into loyalty towards a wider humanity, over and above the ethnocentric loyalty to the group whence he came and in whose values he had been educated.

---

[3] Dag Hammarskjöld, "A Room of Quiet – The United Nations Mediation Room". Leaflet for visitors, 1957; quoted from Bouman (2005: 199f.).
[4] Retrieved from: http://www.goodreads.com/author/quotes/134585.Beyers_Naud_ No further source is given.

The segregated stands of a sports arena in Bloemfontein 1969. One of many telling images of the Apartheid system.

Faith as Solidarity

One of those people who were provided a forum by the Christian Institute and its SPROCAS (Study Project on Christianity in Apartheid Society) programme was the sociologist Rick Turner, before his works were, like himself, removed from the public sphere of apartheid South Africa. Turner, who was assassinated on 8 January 1978 while serving a banning order, promoted perspectives with which Beyers Naudé could certainly identify to a large degree. In what was perhaps his most relevant collection of essays, Turner had observed:

> … unless we think in Utopian terms about South African society we will not really come to understand how it works today. We will take for granted its inequalities, power relationships and behavior patterns which need to be explained. Nor will we be able to evaluate the society adequately. We will not understand on how many different levels there are alternatives, and so the possibility of choice, and so the possibility of moral judgement. (Turner 1972: 7)

Beyers Naudé, like Turner and so many lesser known South Africans, made choices and lived according to moral decisions. So did Dag Hammarskjöld, though in a different role and under different circumstances. Comparing their convictions, these seemingly different personalities had much in common. Not least, they seemed to share a similar notion of solidarity, guided by empathy. They were loyal to fundamental values in their search for justice. Beyers Naudé once put this idea into the following words:

> How do we affect reconciliation between people who hate each other? How do we handle it in a way that we can truly be reconciled, in a way that we can build together where previously we destroyed? We need to look together at what are the major causes of this conflict: poverty, unemployment, and the situation of marginalized people. What do we do to stand in solidarity with them? [5]

And when Hammarskjöld addressed the students of the University of Lund in southern Sweden (close to the isolated rural homestead in Backåkra he had acquired as a prospective retirement home), he stated:

> The health and strength of a community depend on every citizen's feeling of solidarity with the other citizens, and on his willingness, in the name of this solidarity, to shoulder his part of the burdens and responsibilities of the community. The same is of course true of humanity as a whole. And just [as] it cannot be argued that within a community an economic upper class holds its favored position by virtue of greater ability, as a quality which is, as it were, vested in the group by nature, so it is, of course, impossible to maintain this in regard to nations in their mutual relationships. […]

---

[5] Retrieved from: http://www.doonething.org/heroes/pages-n/naude-quotes.htm. No further source is given.

> We thus live in a world where, no more internationally than nationally, any distinct group can claim superiority in mental gifts and potentialities of development (…) Those democratic ideals which demand equal opportunities for all should be applied also to peoples and races. (…) no nation or group of nations can base its future on a claim of supremacy. (Hammarskjöld 1959: 383 and 384)

Determination with Boundaries

Again, I feel on rather safe ground in assuming that Oom Bey would have agreed. But beyond a similar moral compass with coordinates that pointed in the same direction, both men seemed to share other features, rooted in their personalities. It was said of Hammarskjöld that he at times lacked a sense of reality when it came to what was achievable, also by others, and occasionally erred in his assessments of the people he recruited for tasks mainly on the basis of his spontaneous confidence in them (cf. Urquhart 1972: 549). As Fröhlich (2008: 190) concludes, "much of his success was owing to his firm judgement based on his ethical convictions. The reverse of this was a certain tendency to overestimate the strength of his position and to mistake the political realities of a situation." In an interview, Sture Linnér, one of his closest staff members during the 1950s, described this aspect of Hammarskjöld's character in these terms:

> Hammarskjöld's ethical capacity was both his strength and his weakness. Integrity, honesty and character were the basis for all his work. But at the same time he could not understand some procedures of power politics. He could not understand and would not believe that people should be dishonest on very sincere matters and he got indignant about lying. So in a way he was too trusting. (Fröhlich 2008: 190f.)

Similarly, Burnell (2013: 314) alerts us with reference to the works by Ryan (1990) and Villa-Vicencio (1985) that "Naudé was described as stubbornly independent and at times over-enthusiastic about ideas that were impractical. He was also said to have been a poor judge of human character due to his acceptance of people and he would often be let down by them." One of his weaknesses seems to have been, as van der Riet (2013:

Beyers Naudé and Dag Hammarskjöld both came from families with strong political traditions at top level. Beyers Naudé's father Jozua François Naudé (to the left) was Acting Head of State in South Africa from 1967 to 1968. Dag Hammarskjöld's father Hjalmar Hammarskjöld (to the right) was Prime Minister of Sweden from 1914 to 1917.

51) with reference to Heaney (2004: 263) observes, "the trust he sometimes foolishly placed in others." This suggests another striking parallel: Naudé and Hammarskjöld had even more in common than their convictions. Or rather, the related convictions also shaped similar approaches to and interactions with others.

It seems that as both went about their respective "missions" they at times lacked the ability to make realistic judgments about the limitations and weaknesses of others – and maybe even failed to assess their own limitations. Driven by their convictions, they tended to react too much under the influence of their own coordinates, unaware that the coordinates of others were not the same, even when they appeared so at first sight. There was at times an element of self-righteousness or missionary zeal, a characteristic often shared by persons who are visionaries and, as is frequently the case, also marginalised. They tend to end up in isolation as a result of their relentless efforts to place a mirror in front of others, so reminding those others of their imperfections.

Faith as Politics of Hope

Placing Naudé and Hammarskjöld in a similar league, as these few comparisons have tried to do, seems to be a compliment to both. For them, faith was politics, and politics required faith. Their approaches at times even amounted to politics as faith. At the same time, such politics was always also a politics of hope. Hope was the source of strength guiding their engagements. But it was always a hope that was not restricted to parts of humanity. It was an all-embracing hope, which considered others and their living circumstances. As Russel Botman stressed at Beyers Naudé's funeral: "There is no real hope for the son of the farmer unless there is hope in the heart of the daughter of the farmworker." [6]

Despite many setbacks, frustrations and at times even possible moments of despair, Naudé and Hammarskjöld remained beacons of hope throughout their lives, nurtured by their faith in humanity as a source for continued engagement against all the odds. As the transcript of extemporaneous remarks by Hammarskjöld at a United Nations Correspondents' Association Luncheon in his honour on 9 April 1958 reveals, he maintained a "belief and the faith that the future will be all right because there will always be enough people to fight for such a decent future" (quoted in Falkman 2005: 51). Oom Bey would certainly have been among those people in the eyes of Hammarskjöld.

But hope and engagement also required a firm belief, guided by courage. Hammarskjöld once noted that "it is when we all play safe that we create a world of the utmost insecurity. It is when we all play safe that fatality will lead us to our doom. It is 'in the dark shade of courage' alone, that the spell can be broken" (Hammarskjöld 1956b: 142).[7] Such courage also included the willingness to embark on a journey into the unknown as an integral part of the long journey within.

---

[6] Tribute to Beyers Naudé. Unpublished paper delivered at the Memorial Service of Beyers Naudé. Stellenbosch, 18 September 2004; quoted by van der Riet (2013: 125).
[7] The quote is from Ezra Pound, The Cantos, Canto XC.

Part of what the late Norwegian theologian and politician Inge Lønning qualified as "the Reader's Digest version" of Hammarskjöld's legacy holds true for both protagonists:

> 2. Common standards for judgment on how power is exercised could only be moral standards, resting on common human morality, expressed with unbearable accuracy in the sentence "We regard it as self evident that all men are created equal" (The preamble to the United States' Declaration of Independence, 1776).
>
> 3. The principle of the equal dignity of all human beings is the indispensable presupposition for the idea of human rights, which has its complement in the recognition of human obligations, in condensed form expressed in the commandment of love.
>
> 4. To be a durable guiding star for the world of politics the triangle of human dignity/human rights/human obligation needs to be strengthened by the recognition of mankind as a community of shared responsibility and shared guilt, expressed in the shortest possible formula in St. Paul's statement, "For all have sinned and come short of the Glory of god" (Romans 3,23).
>
> 5. Morality, regardless of whether it is brought to awareness of the individual or not, has a religious dimension. Among models of ethical reflection a renewal of the ancient ethics of virtue would be the most promising alternative to take care of that dimension, which is indispensable as a bulwark against the pitfall of moralism. (Lønning 2010: 35f.)

Towards True Humanity

Knowing where to come from and where to go to was a similar source of inspiration for both men. This knowledge served as a point of departure and a home base on the journey into the unknown. Both never denied their roots. Being an Afrikaner in "bone and marrow," as Oom Bey was described by Nelson Mandela (van Kessel 1997: 5), Naudé, like Hammarskjöld the international civil servant who never abandoned his Swedish background,[8] was rooted in an identity, which gave him the security to engage with (real or perceived) otherness. This provided the coordinates to embark on explorations beyond the narrow limits of group imprisonment. It allowed for an open-minded, curious search for the varieties of humanity, explorations that served the similar purpose of belief in a better world, a world that offers a decent living for all free of discrimination and prejudice, no matter where people come from.

Maybe the most rewarding recognition of what Oom Bey and his life-long partner

---

[8] The blueprint for Hammarskjöld's perspectives embedded in his socialisation was best summed up at the beginning of his Secretary-Generalship in his thoughts written for Edward R. Murrow's widely acknowledged radio programme "This I believe," in which he describes faith as "a state of the mind and the soul" (Falkman 2005: 58).

Beyers and Ilse in their garden in Hoylake Road, Greenside, Johannesburg. The photo was taken during Beyer's years of being banned and house arrested, between 1977 and 1984.

Ilse stood and stand for came from the late Madiba:

> Standing in the tradition of great Afrikaners and Patriots like Bram Fischer, Betty Du Toit and others, his life is a shining beacon to all South Africans – both Black and White. It demonstrates what it means to rise above race, to be a true South African. If someone asks me what kind of a person a New South African should be, I will say: Take a look at Beyers and his wife Ilse. [9]

On 3 December 1960, less than a year before his untimely death, Dag Hammarskjöld entered the only rhymed poem in his notebook. It reads in one English translation as follows and might have been wholeheartedly subscribed to by Beyers Naudé: [10]

> "The way,
> You shall follow it.
> Success,
> You shall forget it.
> The cup,
> You shall empty it.
> The pain,
> You shall conceal it.

---

[9] Speech by President Nelson Mandela at the celebration of Beyers Naudé's 80th birthday in 1995 (retrieved from http://robt.shepherd.tripod.com/beyers.html), quoted in Burnell (2013: 319).

[10] This is the translation offered by Erling (2011: 259), which deviates from the one by W.H. Auden (Hammarskjöld 1983: 177).

> The answer,
> You shall learn it.
> The end,
> You shall endure it."

This should not be misunderstood as capitulation to resignation. It should be seen as another form of determination to walk the path, in the firm belief that this is the justified way. Hammarskjöld, according to Bouman (2014: 83), "argued that scepticism towards progress in history could be overcome through spirituality and inspiration by faith." As he stated in his speech to students at Stanford University:

> Whatever doubts history may cast, I believe that the hope for a world of peace and order, inspired by respect for man, has never ceased to agitate the minds of men. I believe that it accounts for the great and noble human spirit behind the ravaged exterior of a history whose self-inflicted wounds have become more and more atrocious. (Hammarskjöld 1955: 512)

Beyers Naudé, like Dag Hammarskjöld and many more, stood for such ideals, beliefs and convictions – and lived accordingly. The values of these two men have survived their worldly lifespan. What Erling Eidem, Archbishop of Sweden, observed at the funeral of Dag Hammarskjöld (as quoted in Urquhart 1972: 597), holds true for Beyers Naudé (and others) as well:

> […] death forces us to face the old and always so disturbing question of the meaning and fulfillment of our life on earth. The answer may be expressed in one word, serve – so measurelessly simple, yet so overwhelmingly filled with significance.

Secretary-General Dag Hammarskjöld arriving at Njili Airport in Leopoldville, Democratic Republic of the Congo, on 13th September, five days before his death. On his left side Prime Minister Cyrille Adoula and, further to the left, General Joseph Mobutu.

References

Gisela Albrecht (2004), "Gehorsam gegenüber Gott," *der überblick*, vol. 40, no. 4, pp. 98-102

Monica Bouman (2005), *Dag Hammarskjöld – Citizen of the World*. Kampen: Ten Have

Monica Bouman (2014), "Dag Hammarskjöld and the Politics of Hope." In: Carsten Stahn and Henning Melber (eds), *Peace Diplomacy, Global Injustice and International Agency. Rethinking Human Security and Ethics in the Spirit of Dag Hammarskjöld*. Cambridge: Cambridge University Press, pp. 77-105

Barbara Burnell (2013), *The Life of Beyers Naudé: A psychobiographical study*. Thesis submitted for Philosophiae Doctor in Psychology, Faculty of Humanities, University of the Free State, July 2013

Murray Coetzee, Retief Muller and Len Hansen (eds) (2015), *Cultivating Seeds of Hope. Conversations on the Life of Beyers Naudé*. Stellenbosch: Stellenbosch University Press

Bernhard Erling (2011), *A Reader's Guide to Dag Hammarskjöld's Waymarks*. Uppsala: Dag Hammarskjöld Foundation <http://www.daghammarskjold.se/publication/readers-guide-dag-hammarskjolds-waymarks/>

Kai Falkman (ed.) (2005), *To Speak for the World. Speeches and Statements by Dag Hammarskjöld*. Stockholm: Atlantis

Manuel Fröhlich (2008), *Political Ethics and the United Nations. Dag Hammarskjöld as Secretary-General*. London and New York: Routledge

Dag Hammarskjöld (1954), "Address before the Second Assembly of the World Council of Churches," Evanston, Illinois, 20 August 1954. UN Press Release SG/393, August 20, 1954; *United Nations Review*, vol. 1, no. 4 (October 1954). In: *Public Papers of the Secretaries-General of the United Nations. Volume II. Dag Hammarskjöld 195-195*. Selected and edited with Commentary by Andrew W. Cordier and Wilder Foote. New York and London: Columbia University Press 19, pp. 351-6

Dag Hammarskjöld (1955), "The World and the Nation" – Commencement Address at Stanford University, Palo Alto, California, June 19, 1955. UN Press Release SG/426, June 18, 1955. In: *Public Papers of the Secretaries-General of the United Nations. Volume II. Dag Hammarskjöld 1953-1956*. Selected and edited with Commentary by Andrew W. Cordier and Wilder Foote. New York and London: Columbia University Press 1972, pp. 508-13

Dag Hammarskjöld (1956a), "The United Nations – Its Ideology and Activities," Address before the Indian Council of World Affairs, New Delhi, India, February 3, 1956. UN Department of Public Information Pamphlet, April, 1956. In: *Public Papers of the Secretaries-General of the United Nations. Volume II. Dag Hammarskjöld 1953-1956*. Selected and edited with Commentary by Andrew W. Cordier and Wilder Foote. New York and London: Columbia University Press 1972, pp. 658-73

Dag Hammarskjöld (1956b), "Address at Celebration of the 180th Anniversary of the Virginia Declaration of Rights," Williamsburg, Virginia, May 15, 1956. UN Press Release SG/479, May 14, 1956. In: *Public Papers of the Secretaries-General of the United Nations. Volume III. Dag Hammarskjöld 1956-1957*. Selected and edited with Commentary by Andrew W. Cordier and Wilder Foote. New York and London: Columbia University Press 1973, pp. 137-42

Dag Hammarskjöld (1956c), "On the Uppsala Tradition – From Address after Receiving Honorary Degree at Upsala College, East Orange, N.J., June 4, 1956. UN Press Release SG/484/Rev. 1, June 4, 1956. In: *Public Papers of the Secretaries-General of the United Nations. Volume III. Dag Hammarskjöld 1956-1957.* Selected and edited with Commentary by Andrew W. Cordier and Wilder Foote. New York and London: Columbia University Press 1973, pp. 164-5

Dag Hammarskjöld (1959), "Asia, Africa, and the West." Address Before the Academic Association of the University of Lund. Lund, Sweden, May 4, 1959. UN Press Release SG/813, May 4, 1959. In: *Public Papers of the Secretaries-General of the United Nations. Volume IV: Dag Hammarskjöld 1958-1960.* Selected and edited with Commentary by Andrew W. Cordier and Wilder Foote. New York and London: Columbia University Press 1974, pp. 380-7

Dag Hammarskjöld (1983), *Markings.* New York: Ballantine (Swedish original 1963; English first published 1964)

Michael John Heaney (2004), *Beyers Naudé, ekumeniese baanbreker in Suid Afria 1960-1994.* PhD thesis in Philosophy, Theological Faculty/University of Pretoria

Roger Lipsey (2013), *Hammarskjöld. A Life.* Ann Arbor: University of Michigan Press

Inge Lønning (2010), "Politics, Morality and Religion – The Legacy of Dag Hammarskjöld." In: Hans Corell/Inge Lønning/Henning Melber, *The Ethics of Dag Hammarskjöld.* Uppsala: Dag Hammarskjöld Foundation, pp. 18-37

Henning Melber (2014), "The death of Dag Hammarskjöld," *Review of African Political Economy,* vol. 41, no. 141, pp. 458-65

Chris Saunders (2011), "Dag Hammarskjöld and Apartheid South Africa." In: Henning Melber/Maxi Schoeman (eds), *The United Nations and Regional Challenges in Africa – 50 Years After Dag Hammarskjöld.* Uppsala: Dag Hammarskjöld Foundation (development dialogue, no. 57), pp. 61-75

Tor Sellström (ed.) (1999), *Liberation in Southern Africa – Regional and Swedish Voices.* Uppsala: Nordiska Afrikainstitutet

Tor Sellström (2011), "Hammarskjöld and apartheid South Africa: Mission unaccomplished," *African Journal on Conflict Resolution,* vol. 11, no. 1, pp. 35-62

Colleen Ryan (1990), *Beyers Naudé. Pilgrimage of Faith.* Cape Town: David Phillip

Richard Turner (1972), *The Eye of the Needle. An Essay on Participatory Democracy.* Johannesburg: Study Project for Christianity in Apartheid Society (SPROCAS 2)

Brian Urquhart (1972), *Hammarskjold.* New York: Norton

Ryno Louis van der Riet (2013), *Beyers Naudé: Advocate of hope? A historical theological reading of his public addresses.* Master of Theology Thesis, Faculty of Theology, Stellenbosch University

Ineke van Kessel (1997), "Beyers Naudé: Afrikaner in merg en been. 'Natuurlijk ben ik vaak woedend geweest'," *Zuidelijk Afrika,* no. 4, pp. 4-5

Charles Villa-Vicencio (1985), "A life of resistance and hope." In: Charles Villa-Vicencio/John W. De Gruchy (eds.), Resistance and hope. *South African essays in honour of Beyers Naudé.* Cape Town: David Philip, pp. 3-13

Rhodesian volunteers leaving Salisbury for service in the war 1899.

Ecumenical Witness for Social Justice: Beyers Naudé and Denis Hurley for our Times [1]

N. Barney Pityana

The Great South African War (1899-1902) ended in a great betrayal for the indigenous peoples of South Africa. What happened was that two European settler communities shared the spoils of a war to which the owners of the land were not party and whose interests were not a factor in the war in the first place. Boer and British parcelled out the land and wealth of the country among themselves and the Africans were no consideration in the constitutional arrangements agreed to at the Treaty of Vereeniging that ended the hostilities. In other words, the peace was between Boer and Brit, and the African indigenous people were never to be at peace with the invaders. Arguably, the Boers, although they may have lost the battle, won the war. They got to retain political power under the British Empire on terms that specifically excluded virtually all Africans and many Coloured people from the franchise. That arrangement became the substance of the Union of South Africa in 1910.

---

[1] This is based on the Dr Beyers Naudé and Archbishop Denis E. Hurley OMI Lecture to mark the centenary of the birth of the two stalwarts of the church in South Africa, given at the Denis Hurley Centre, Durban, 10 May 2015.

But to some Boer generals this was a hard pill to swallow because it meant that the erstwhile Boer Republics were no more. Insurgencies ensued, and the *bittereinders* with their "never-say-die" determination under Generals de la Rey, de Wet and Beyers mounted rebellions in the Western Transvaal in 1914. General C.F. Beyers was the commander under whom J.F. Naudé, the father of Beyers Naudé, served in the war. Beyers was as deeply religious and conservative as they come, resentful of the bullying by the British, and determined to restore the dignity of the Afrikaners, preserve their culture, establish their language and, in time, assure self-determination for the Afrikaner *volk*. He it was after whom the infant Christiaan Frederick Beyers Naudé was named by his parents when he was born on 10 May 1915.

One of the great schemes of Lord Milner at the end of the war, and one which the Treaty of Vereeniging presumed, was that there would be massive British immigration to South Africa that would counteract the dominance of Afrikaners in the British colonies as well as in the former Boer Republics, and thereby change the political dynamics of the Boer Republics and the new Union of South Africa at large. In general, British immigrants were hardly the cream of society. They were there to relieve Britain of the burden of unemployment, social misfits and gold diggers. They were hardly the material on which British influence and power in South Africa could be built. As it happened, that flood of immigration never materialised and the dominance of Afrikaners remained intact. It may well be that had Alfred, Lord Milner, the high commissioner, been more realistic about the prospects of his plan, he might have looked at an alliance with the native populations differently!

Children of war-time South Africa

For years, the Afrikaners were suspicious of Catholics as the *Roomsche gevaar*, and it is fair to say that Roman Catholics continued to suffer discrimination in the stratified Cape social hierarchy. It is doubtful that the British occupations of 1795 and 1806, prior to the British establishment of a permanent settlement at the Cape in 1812 in response to the Napoleonic Wars, changed much in Dutch laws and social and religious arrangements. Roman Catholic missions and immigration were never encouraged. When Denis Hurley was born on 9 November 1915, he would have been born into a climate of discrimination and suspicion against his Irish Catholic immigrant family. His father was the keeper of the lighthouse at Cape Point – a lowly, humble and lonely occupation if ever there was one, but critical for the safety of the maritime traffic along the busy routes around the Cape.

It is the irony of our times that it was to two such unlikely personalities as Beyers Naudé and Denis Hurley that South Africa and the church owe so much. Unlikely because they were drawn from the opposite ends of the spectrum: class and privilege; religion, language and culture; as well as the geographical divides, with all that meant for attitudes and political assumptions, Cape liberals and Transvaal Afrikaner nationalists. Yet both were children of war-time South Africa, a country thrust into the First World War in defence of the Empire but with deeply divided loyalties. The first of the so-called World Wars was a war against Germany, and the Union of South Africa, as part of the British Empire, was thrust into active participation in the war. Three events are worth noting as more or less contemporaneous with the birth of these great South Africans.

Conflict over the "Native Problem"

In 1912, the South African Native Congress was formed. It was to be the vehicle for expressing the demands of the African peoples of the new Union, whose voice was never sought in national affairs and whose rights had been bargained away by the settler community. No sooner was Congress formed than the new government enacted the Native Land Act of 1913 giving legal effect to a history of incremental dispossession of African people from land ownership, as well as creating reserves or territories into which Africans were to be herded. Those who sacrificed most in the war were the African troopers who enlisted, encouraged by the emerging leadership of the fledgling struggle in the hope that the political claims of the African people would be addressed sympathetically by the British Empire. On 21 February 1917, 607 troops of the South African Labour Corps perished at sea aboard the *SS Mendi* steamship en route to the frontline in France. They received no recognition, no medals and no mention for bravery. A great injustice was done to those who paid the ultimate sacrifice.

It was into such a society that these figures of South African history came to life. They would have been immersed in the contradictions of their time; a society deeply divided along racial lines, and a privileged class of white European heritage that was forever at war with itself; a society in Africa but to varying degrees never quite comfortable about being African or embracing the African identity – in Africa and yet preoccupied with fighting the unfinished battles of Europe on African soil. At the margins of all this were the African people. They were not the centre of concern, but their subaltern presence and being could never be ignored. Indeed, in time, it was to be proved that South African governance and politics were dictated by conflict over the "Native Problem." Both Beyers Naudé and Denis Hurley were ordinary white South Africans – lived a life of separation where prejudice across all societal divides was predominant, and whose competing interests somehow had to be reconciled, or were under constant challenge.

Through the lens of these two great South Africans, I propose to take a snapshot through 100 years of Christian social witness for justice in South Africa. I ask the question that with all the changes that have happened in our country, what prophetic witness is appropriate or called for from the church of our times?

A young Denis Hurley

Photo: Denis Hurley Center

Reverend Fred van Wigh and Beyers Naudé in Cottesloe, Johannesburg, December 1960. The Cottesloe Statement was the outcome of a consultation conference arranged by the *World Council of Churches* in 1960, as a reaction to the Sharpeville massacre. The statement rejected discrimination in various forms.

Beyers Naudé

Beyers Naudé was a man of Afrikaner stock through and through. His father, Jozua Francois Naudé, was a *dominee* in the Dutch Reformed Church, of Voortrekker lineage, saw service in the Boer War and served the church dutifully. The desire of the family was that their children would be their pride and truly embrace the Afrikaner identity and consciousness. Beyers Naudé himself imbibed these ideas dutifully, graduated from Stellenbosch, was ordained a minister of the Dutch Reformed Church and served the church in various capacities.

There are perhaps two significant character traits that were to define the destiny of Beyers Naudé: he was a man of faith, and he was perceptive and discerning. Once he came to faith, faith took over. It was faith that dictated his life. It was difficult to move him once he came to an understanding of faith as God's will. It was in that regard that he was rooted in the Reformed Calvinist theology and spirituality that viewed the Bible as the inerrant Word of God. Even those who disagreed with Beyers Naudé readily acknowledged his unshakeable belief in the God of the Bible. It was because of his belief in God that he embraced the aspirations of the Afrikaner people, and he imbibed the biblical theology of Afrikaner nationalism.

The second characteristic is that he was perceptive and deeply thoughtful. It is not suggested here that he was in any formal or intellectual sense a deep thinker, otherwise he might be regarded as calculating and cautious. He was not. He was sensitive enough to discern with the eye of faith what went below the surface and beyond the obvious. His sensitivity was such that he asked questions, awkward questions, of himself, of his teachers and of God. To that extent he was an anxious and restless enquirer. His curiosity was such that nothing was taken for granted, or was beyond probing. Even when he was quiet, his mind was at work cogitating on what some might simply have dismissed as irrelevant. My contention, then, is that for *Oom Bey* conversion was never a "sudden experience." It was the culmination of years of questions and doubt, and tentative exploration of ideas – a kind of chewing the cud!

The Sharpeville Massacre

For many of us it was Sharpeville, the first massacre by the Afrikaner Nationalist government since it came to power in 1948 of black people, who were in this case protesting against the pass laws. Sixty-nine of them were killed, and that caused international outrage. But that does not explain why Sharpeville had such an impact on him, given the propaganda he would have been subjected to, and his responsibilities as a pastor to counsel his own congregation during times of tension in society. Some say that this was the result of the questions his young missionary pastors posed him based on their own pastoral situations in the daughter churches. But why would he have taken any interest in their questions, given what the church was teaching? Evidently, questions arose for him because his mind was at work testing the biblical evidence against the social and political context he was confronted with.

Archbishop Denis Hurley refers to Beyers Naudé as a man of conversion. We sometimes talk about conversion as a Damascus Road experience, a bolt from the blue, a sudden, paralysing encounter with God. Conversion, however, arises from one's faith experience and an honest engagement with all the questions that it raises. It also requires a will and a mind that trusts God and is obedient to God. It requires the courage of one's convictions and a sacrificial self-giving of oneself. To this extent, Beyers Naudé could have drawn inspiration from Pope Benedict XVI's often quoted dictum that,

THE SHARPEVILLE MASSACRE. After a day of demonstrations in the township of Sharpeville, just south of Johannesburg, on 21 March 1960, a crowd of about 5,000 to 7,000 black protesters went to the police station. The police opened fire on the crowd, killing 69 people. Photos of the massacre were spread by anti-apartheid movements all over the world, as here on a lobby of Parliament organised by the British anti-apartheid movement in 1965 when it printed 30,000 of these postcards for supporters to send to the Prime Minister.

"being a Christian is not the result of an ethical choice or a lofty idea, but the encounter with an event, a person, which gives life a new horizon and a decisive direction."

Facing up to his Moderature

For Beyers Naudé, it was the study of scripture that informed his ideas about God, who dictated one's actions and life. That was the reason he could not, in good conscience, withdraw his initial and informed endorsement of the Cottesloe Statement, even as some of his fellow delegates, one by one, were put under pressure to do so. As moderator of the Southern Transvaal Synod, he had the courage to stand alone at synod and refuse to denounce the Cottesloe Statement in the absence of any Biblical evidence to the contrary for doing so.

That is the reason he could face up to his Moderature, which demanded that he resign as editor of *Pro Veritate*; and that was the reason he was graceful in accepting the authority of the church even as he disagreed with it, resigned his calling as minister of the Aasvöelkop kerk, and symbolically disrobed himself when he had preached his valedictory sermon to his congregation in 1963. That is the reason he opted to continue as director of the Christian Institute rather than face life as a caged bird in relative comfort within the church. The truth that Beyers Naudé's life portends up to this point was that of obedience to God: hence Acts 5:29 was his text for his valedictory sermon at Aaselvöel NGK *gemeente*. His diligence in searching the Scriptures led him to the discovery that the theological claims of Afrikaner nationalism were false. This laid the foundations for the eventual collapse of the theological myth on which Afrikaner nationalism had been predicated for so long.

Pro Veritate was the monthly journal of the Christian Institute of Southern Africa from 1962 to 1977. Beyers Naudé was the editor. The journal was banned in 1977.

But God was not done with Beyers Naudé. He was outside the church of his birth, but it never left him in his being and consciousness. His convictions about the Reformation inspired by John Calvin were unshaken. That remained his guiding light through difficult times. He was able to apply that faith in his ecumenical work, especially his recognition of freedom in the spirit. What it also did was to free him to understand more deeply the plight of Black people in South Africa, and to work within the church for justice.

> "Peter and the apostles answered, we must obey God rather than men"
>
> – Acts of the Apostles 5:29

Identifying with the oppressed

The Christian Institute became a key structure of the ecumenical movement in South Africa, alongside the South African Council of Churches (SACC) and the Roman Catholic Church. As a body of individual participants, the Christian Institute brought Christians and enquirers together around the study of the Bible, across all racial and language divides, without having to defer to any ecclesiastical dogma, but guided only by the Christian convictions of the participants. It became, in the words of Liberation Theology, a base ecclesial formation or cell. It could help develop people to become prophetic voices in their own communities, to develop into change agents as part of a vast developmental network.

The Christian Institute soon became an attraction to many, especially from the Dutch Reformed Churches, not least because evidently everyone was treated with respect and equally. Its programmes also expanded, embracing the vast community of independent or indigenous churches that had been marginalised for so long among mainline churches. It also began to work among women and rural communities. The Christian Institute also supported the activities of anti-apartheid organisations, especially among students like the National Union of South African Students (NUSAS) and the South African Students' Organisation (SASO).

Leaflet from the US American anti-apartheid movement *Episcopal Churchmen for South Africa* condemning the banning of the Christian Institute and its magazine Pro Veritate, November 1977. African Activist Archive, USA.

For me, though, there was nothing significant about all that. The true revolutionary work of Beyers Naudé was at the time when the struggle was intensifying and repression was at its worst. It was then that Naudé and the Christian Institute were banned, and it was then that Naudé perhaps experienced the worst forms of oppression that identified him with the oppressed, the enemy of *Afrikanerdom* – and that must have cut deep! He was the one who understood the message of Black Consciousness when many were sceptical or afraid. He opened his heart to those who were banned like he was, and in time, he could serve as a contact for the underground operatives who trusted him. As general secretary of the SACC, he continued the work that took root during John Rees's time as general secretary, and which grew significantly during the time that Bishop (as he was then) Desmond Tutu took over the reins as general secretary in 1978 as resistance to apartheid was escalating: the Dependants' Conference to provide material support to the families of political prisoners and families of detainees. He also continued the work that his friend Dr Wolfram Kistner undertook at the Justice and Reconciliation Desk – painstaking research, documentation and information-gathering and dissemination on apartheid and its effects on human rights and justice for the poor.

Tambo and Naudé embracing

During the times of internal conflict, Beyers Naudé stood with those who sought to overthrow the apartheid system. He was never neutral. He also supported conscientious objection by young white men who faced conscription into the apartheid armed forces, and, in the end, he was ready to make overtures to the ANC in exile because he was confident that there could be no solution to the political crisis in the country without the ANC participating on its own terms. Thus it came as a surprise to many that Nelson Mandela included Beyers Naudé in his delegation to meet the South African government at Groote Schuur, an event that produced the Groote Schuur Minute.[2] "The stone that the builders rejected has become the head of the corner."

My most abiding memory is of the consultation in Lusaka, Zambia in May 1987 by the Programme to Combat Racism (PCR). The consultation brought together church leaders and the liberation movements to consider proposals for the resolution of the South African conflict. In effect, it was a gathering between the churches in South Africa with the liberation movements. Other churches as well as the solidarity movement were also in attendance. Oliver Tambo was the main speaker. I remember how uncanny it was when Tambo, in the middle of reading his paper, stopped, took off his glasses, and recognised Oom Bey seated in the front row. He put his paper down, descended to approach Beyers Naudé to greet him – and then these two men embraced, to the applause of the conference. They had never met before, but they recognised the significance of that moment. The conference adopted the Lusaka Statement, which was a ground-breaking statement on the illegitimacy of the apartheid state and the legitimacy of armed struggle. But most memorable to many was that encounter and recognition between these two great South Africans.

"I salute you my brother - whom I have never seen before - with respect and admiration". Oliver Tambo meeting Beyers Naudé for the first time at the World Council of Churches' meeting in Lusaka, Zambia, 4-8 May 1987.

Denis Hurley

There is an uncanny resemblance between these two characters of the South African church, and yet also some contrasts. Archbishop Denis E. Hurley OMI was a man of the church through and through. He was to have an important role to play in the

---

[2] Entered into on 4 May 1990 in Cape Town, whereby the government and the ANC agreed on a common commitment to address the existing climate of violence and intimidation from whatever quarter, as well as to stability and a peaceful process of negotiations.

Durban 1941. Denis Hurley blessing ambulance with Bishop Henri Delalle.

Impatient about slow progress

Fr Smangaliso Mkatshwa (2001) remembers him as a very pastoral bishop, strong in guiding the Catholic Bishops' Conference in its statements against apartheid, but not doing enough to advance Black priests in the church. Though he was known to be independent-minded and was critical of the record of the church on social issues especially apartheid, he remained till the end a very loyal prelate, ready to defend the church's record against critics within and without. And yet he was strong in engaging and debating with church activists, and in insisting on order against disruptive behaviour. In that respect, he was never patronising towards Black radicals. He challenged them, including Mkatshwa, and pressed the case of the church against its critics. He caused them to argue their case, listened attentively and explained in a manner that they would understand and accept. In that respect, Hurley was an unlikely advocate of the church – for some, that stance could undermine his credibility, but it never did so.

He was impatient about the slow progress of the Catholic Bishops' Conference on social issues, especially in raising its voice against apartheid, but he made it clear, as Mkatshwa soon discovered, that he was prepared to defend the church against some wayward radicals within it.

To that extent, therefore, it is fair to say that Vatican II was for the Archbishop of Durban a conversion experience,

THE SECOND VATICAN COUNCIL, informally known as Vatican II, took place in 1962-1965 and reformed the Catholic Church.

1980s Black Sash Protest. Denis Hurley outside the General Post Office in Durban.

as much as it was for the Catholic Church. The wake-up call, though, came from the events from Sharpeville 1960 to Soweto 1976. This was a time of enormous turmoil and repression by the apartheid state: it is referred to in his collection of papers edited by Denis Philippe as a time of crisis. In the 1980s, the campaigns of ungovernability put the church in a place where it could no longer be detached from the struggles of the people and had to make some uncomfortable choices. The rising deaths in detention meant that the pastoral resources of the church were in demand, and so was its prophetic voice.

He was no Colenso

I believe that Vatican II did two things that were indispensable for the church in South Africa. First, it liberated the church to understand its evangelical mission as a community of faith in the world. Archbishop Denis Hurley called this the conversion of the church. "The Pastoral Constitution of the Church in the Modern World," *Gaudium et Spes*, promulgated by Pope Paul VI on 7 December 1965 right at the end of the Council opens with the magisterial words that seemed to penetrate to the heart of the pastoral conditions then prevailing in South Africa: "The joys and hopes, the griefs and the anxieties of men of this age, especially those who are poor or in any way afflicted, these are the joys and hopes, the griefs and anxieties of the followers of Christ."

Rev Joe Fourie, Bishop Stanley Mogoba (Methodist), Archbishop Denis Hurley OMI (Roman Catholic), Bishop Michael Nuttall (Anglican) and Bishop John Borman (Methodist) leading the 20,000 strong march to Durban City Hall on 26 September 1990 as part of the Defiance Campaign.

The theology of Vatican II became, for Archbishop Hurley, his principal pastoral and teaching duty in his episcopate from then onwards. It informed his thinking about the world, and the church, and it shaped his bias towards the poor, and his increasingly voluble campaigns against apartheid. It surely could have been no mean act of bravery to make a silent witness outside the main Post Office in Durban on 15 December 1976 with a placard to draw attention to deaths in detention, and to those in detention without trial, or his advocacy of a signature campaign to draw attention to the evil of detention without trial in 1984. These acts placed his archiepiscopal authority behind the efforts to awaken conscience about injustice and placed the church alongside those who suffered persecution for righteousness's sake (Denis 1997: 213).

Elsewhere, Liberation Theology advanced rapidly and a great deal of theological contextualisation and experimentation became possible, though it was never explicitly welcome in the Roman curia due to anxieties in sections of the church hierarchy about the possibility of maintaining authority over the teachings of the church. *Gaudium et Spes* gave to the church armoury the socio-analytical method in theology, that the "signs of the times were to be interpreted in the light of the gospel."

JOHN WILLIAM COLENSO (1814–1883), British theologian who came to South Africa in 1853, recruited as first bishop of Natal. He devoted the latter years of his life as an advocate for native Africans who had been unjustly treated by the colonial regime.

The Vatican Council and *Gaudium et Spes* brought about recognition of the church as a universal instrument of salvation. That meant the church recognised that salvation came to God's people in their language and culture and in their own circumstances or contexts. In this way, the church was freed to reckon with the place of culture in the propagation of the gospel. This also set in place a movement of inculturation and it resulted, especially in Africa, in a fresh look at African ways of being and believing that had been eclipsed for far too long by Western notions of knowledge and faith practice. Archbishop Hurley was no Colenso, and in that regard does not appear to have played much of a role in the inculturation movement, although he was one of the prime movers in liturgical renewal in the Catholic Church.

Yearning for justice

My final observation is the one that brings the two subjects of my chapter together. In his tribute to Beyers Naudé, Archbishop Hurley combined in Beyers Naudé the notions of the world, catholicity and the gospel. He notes that Naudé was faithful to the gospel, and yet he was rooted in the world that was yearning for justice. His words in his chapter, "Beyers Naudé: Calvinist and Catholic" are apposite:

> The church has a mandate to promote good behavior and right relations between people which are woven of justice and love … The church, without aspiring to political power, has the responsibility of promoting ethical standards in politics and economics as in all other aspects of human behaviour … The church was getting increasingly out of touch with reality. (Randall 1982: 146)

This concern that the church is cloistered and out of touch with its soul and the world it inhabited and was surrounded by, meant that it was incapable of proclaiming the gospel to any effect. Part of being "out there" meant the church had to take risks and abjure any quest for security and certainties. Second, the church had to be courageous in her convictions in obedience to Christ, trusting only in the God of all life.

I imagine that that was what lay behind Archbishop Hurley's advocacy of ecumenical cooperation, especially in all social matters and in the witness to justice in the world. Thus it is that the Good Friday Procession of Witness in Durban has become a common statement of the churches to this day about the common proclamation of the good news. Thus it was that the Diakonia Council of Churches was established in KwaZulu Natal to bring the churches together to be a common sign of the life we live together in Christ. Archbishop Hurley always advocated for the Catholic Church's involvement in the SACC, first as an observer, but later as a full member.

What Archbishop Hurley had to say in his tribute to Beyers Naudé applies equally to him:

Denis Hurley with pope St John Paul II in 2003.

> Beyers Naudé – an important sign to the churches – a sign of conversion to Christian love in its most demanding dimensions, a sign of justice and transformation, a sign of Christian collaboration across denominational barriers, a sign too of what it means to be both Calvinist and Catholic, a sign of the Cross of Christ and Hope of the Resurrection. (Randall 1982: 152)

South African anomie today

I trust I shall not be making an outlandish statement that seems totally alien to your ears if I observe that we live in very difficult times in our country for church and society. For one thing it is observable that we are in a Season of Discontent, whichever direction one turns – whether it be communities, or sections of communities, protesting the installation of electricity meters in Orlando, Soweto, or elsewhere, and demanding a flat rate for the utility, much against policy and indeed, much against common business practice; or the people of Malamulele or Bekkersdal or Matatiele or Herschel demanding their own municipality regardless of the processes for demarcation of boundaries by the Demarcation Board; or communities aggrieved by one thing or another, setting buildings on fire in a destructive rage, or holding their children back from attending school just because they are demanding that a tarred road be built in their village. Researchers tell us that South Africa has earned a reputation as the protest capital of the world, with at least three protest marches in different parts of the country on any one day, drawing a large number of participants.

All these point to a breakdown in relations between the governed and those who govern. One can note painfully the social malaise that engulfs our society: the escalating instances of women who die at the instance of their husbands or partners; or children, especially girl children, who are victims of sexual abuse at the hands of their own fathers or close relatives; or the prevalence of rape, sometimes of elderly women at the hands of young men or even boys; or witch hunting directed against elderly women or widows. Crime everywhere has just become unmanageable and the criminal justice system definitely is not coping. The ostensibly privileged who are university students are engaged in campaigns for transformation and dialogue against university management that appears to be ineffectual or that has broken down. The prevalent culture of South Africans these days is one of demand, violence and shouting, rather than dialogue, communication and listening to all points of view. South Africans no longer speak the language of dialogue, or listening or hearing, or appreciating one another's points of view. The predominant theme is one of anger, suspicion and rejection.

Targeting the alien in our midst

Thus it is that we have been experiencing wave after wave of xenophobia and attacks against immigrants who live among communities in the townships or villages and who share a common life with the people. The inability to form community, or unwillingness to find a neighbour in the other or a refusal to express *Ubuntu* in our daily dealings with others, is a deep-seated contradiction of what we purport to believe. I have heard surprise and outrage at this development. In reality it is not surprising. It is a curious fact, indeed, that these events occur predominantly among those who are on the fringes of society, among the poor and the unemployed, where there is contestation over scarce resources, and where crime and the fear of crime is rife. That explains that at the drop of a pin, large crowds gather whenever there is commotion – that is because large hordes of people are idle, unemployed, resentful and angry. In a sense, therefore, it is not about a strategic assault on foreigners, except that among the powerless and marginalised they represent an even higher form of vulnerability.

Sociologists will perhaps tell us that South African society has reached a point of anomie. That is when society and individuals in society are no longer certain about themselves and their sense of belonging. They find that the rules of society they had believed in no longer apply or no longer apply to their benefit, as had been expected. Social relationships are fragmented and no longer offer security. To that extent society loses meaning in their lives. Emile Durkheim, the 19th century French sociologist to whom this theory is attributed, tells us that when the situation deteriorates to this extent, we have the makings of social change that is inevitable and already underway.[3]

---

[3] Berger and Berger 1972: 303

The causes of the state of anomie are inevitably those who control the levers of power, whether it be government or business. They have power and the means to impose their will for a time and are not immediately targets of popular anger or revolt. The immediate targets are the vulnerable, the poor, women and children, the alien in our midst or any at the lowest stratum of society. By its nature, anomie is inarticulate, disorganised and un-strategic. It represents frustration short of passing judgment on the powerful and those with means.

The subjects of popular anger

Sadly, in South Africa we have failed to read this sociological analysis. We are targeting the inanimate statues (out of a very partial reading of history and unmindful of the continuing value of learning from history!) rather than addressing the source of the problem; or the migrants who are vulnerable and share the same socioeconomic spaces with the victims; or women and children who are without power. In reality, anomie itself is not revolution. It is unlikely to result in meaningful and lasting change. One never addresses power by attacking those without it. The 2013 Apostolic Exhortation by Pope Francis, *Evangelii Gaudium*, captures for me the kind of situation we find ourselves in in South Africa today:

> The great danger in today's world, pervaded as it is by consumerism, is the desolation and anguish born of a complacent yet covetous heart, the feverish pursuit of frivolous pleasures, and a blunted conscience. Whenever our interior life becomes caught up in its own interests and concerns, there is no longer room for others, no place for the poor. God's voice is no longer heard, the quiet joy of his love is no longer felt, and the desire to do good fades. This is a very real danger for believers too. Many fall prey to it, and end up resentful, angry and listless.

Put this way, the challenge of our society today is a challenge for the church. That must surely explain the obscene materialism, selfishness and greed that blinds our country, alongside abject poverty and inequality; or the excessive debt that so many South Africans are prey to; or the violence and crime that is about grabbing and killing for that which someone else has; or the continuous and insatiable desire to have more and more (often without deserving) is at the root of so many of our social problems.

Stellenbosch theologian Elna Mouton in an article on "Christian Theology at the University" situates this societal malaise in postmodernist thinking – that elevation and privileging of the individual to the exclusion of everyone else. In her view, this:

> … leads to a breakdown of the hegemony of truth claims. Instead of celebrating the richness of plurality and complementarity, of sharing one another's identities and stories of joy and pain (which I believe is what postmodern thinking is about), the postmodern attitude for many becomes synonymous with a certain *disintegration*, with a loss of orientation and cohesion, the loss of a collective moral identity, memory and destination, and consequently, the *loss* of a

corresponding (corporate) ethos of dignity and respect for life, of responsibility and involvement, with a general attitude of "who cares?" (Mouton 2008: 439)

For many, this means a loss of trust in all forms of leadership – including church leadership. Due to such detached and uninterested attitudes, extreme postmodernist thinking necessarily fails to cultivate a sustainable agenda for transformation. That is a wake-up call. It means that society in general has lost trust and confidence in those pillars of life in society – church and politics. Authority is under challenge because leadership has failed the people. Looked at that way, the real subjects of popular anger are not so much the poor and vulnerable, but the powerful, and the resentment is against those who occupy leadership. This has the makings of both an authoritarian state and a revolution, as Hannah Arendt points out.[4]

Likewise, one can tune in to the existentialism associated with French philosopher Jean Paul Sartre and recognise that far from the modern people being confident about themselves and taking charge of their lives, there is a sense of, and fear of, drift and formlessness. It is a disorienting thing not to know where to turn, or to find familiar solutions elusive. Commenting on this condition Ernest Gellner observes that existentialism was at its most pervasive when times were complex and confused, when there was a sense of crisis and "intellectual depression".[5] It is when the anchors of belief systems of authority or certainty no longer provide confidence and one can't fall back on them, that one may well rebel. Looked at that way, it is only fair to say that as South Africans we surely suffer from a sustained collective madness – of a kind that is no different from that which for so many years suffocated us in the madness of apartheid.

To summarise, the challenge South Africa faces is bad government and poor leadership. Somehow we have managed to breed a generation of angry and resentful South Africans, and we would do well to take heed to their voices.

Living the Gospel

One of Pope Francis's memorable sayings is that he yearns for a church that is "bruised, hurting and dirty because it has been on the streets, rather than a church concerned with being at the centre, and then, ends up being caught up in a web of obsessions and procedures" (*Evangelii Gaudium*). That is exactly where Beyers Naudé and Archbishop Denis Hurley OMI felt comfortable. The public proclamation of the gospel in word and deed was for them the imperative. Dr Beyers Naudé was forced to work outside the formal structures of the church, and Archbishop Hurley had to work with patience within the church of his time. For both, however, the idea of missionary discipleship held sway. In South Africa we are very uncomfortable with the idea of a church that is poor, however much we may preach about being the church of the poor. This reminds me of George Bernard Shaw's play, *Major Barbara*, in which he says that it is not the

---

[4] See her popular The Origins of Totalitarianism (1951) and The Human Condition (1956).
[5] Magee 1978: 295

idea that we live with poverty to have relevance. For Shaw, poverty was the worst of crimes. It is rather that as long as there are poor in our midst, our apostolic calling is to be in solidarity with the poor and to struggle with them and in their midst for life. It also means that we have to address constructively all the reasons and structures responsible for the poverty and marginalisation that is dehumanising the great majority of the people of God. Poverty does not just exist as of right, it is caused by unjust structures of society.

It is often the case that whenever the church gets preoccupied with herself and with her minutiae, she loses touch with her missionary discipleship and becomes obsessed with order and discipline, often resulting in internal conflict. When the church does that, it gets lost and no one takes responsibility. When the church is at the market place preaching the gospel, it is in touch with its own essential nature, with its humanity. When that happens, then the church becomes prey to opportunists within and without – political leaders who seek only home-grown palace prophets who prophesy according to the dictates of the Master; or who, in a materialistic world, may be bought and traded to the highest bidder in a transactional relationship with the rich and the powerful. Then the church has lost her soul. When she loses courage to preach the good news, she loses zeal for the House of God and God's people become prey to ravenous lions, all because the shepherd has abandoned her calling.

In our country, I believe we need to recover that analytical capacity and theological depth that marked the contributions of Beyers Naudé and Archbishop Hurley to national dialogues. We should specifically have the courage to say that the economic trajectory our country has chosen is a dangerous delusion, leading us towards market-oriented oblivion. More determined steps are needed to change the way in which this society and its economy are arranged or organised. This economy of exclusion and privilege for the few must be challenged, and at the moral level we must reiterate the four NOs that Pope Francis inveighs against with such effect in *Evangelii Gaudium*: No to the economy of exclusion; No to the idolatry of money; No to the financial system that rules rather than saves; No to inequality that spawns violence. There is a need for a more compassionate and moral ethic that does not sacrifice the lives of ordinary citizens at the altar of capital and greed. I believe that we can have no gospel to proclaim unless and until we ourselves in the church actually live the gospel we proclaim. That is what our two centenarians bequeathed us, our church and our society.

What I fear most about our society today is a culture of compromise with evil, a failure to challenge wrongdoing because we have become too comfortable in it and cannot imagine a future without it, and we fear to let our voices be heard and the truth is blunted. I fear that we are being herded like cattle into a state of dangerous acquiescence. It is the rebel in Beyers Naudé and Archbishop Hurley that we should draw inspiration from, that we may have the courage to interrogate received wisdom, make those in power accountable, articulate our constitutional values and make evil uncomfortable in our midst. Oxford philosopher Sir Isaiah Berlin has prescient words for us:

> If the imagination is to be stirred, if the intellect is to work, if mental life is not to sink to a low ebb, and the pursuit of truth (or justice, or self-fulfilment) is not to cease, assumptions must be questioned, presuppositions must be challenged – sufficiently … to keep society moving. (Magee 1978: 17)

That is the reason that our country is in dire need of an ecumenical vision for social justice, and ecumenical leaders who cannot be corrupted or bought off, and a church that is resilient in the face of harsh challenges from erstwhile friends.

Sources

Peter and Brigitte Berger (1972), *Sociology: A Biographical Approach*. New York: Basic Books

Philippe Denis (ed.) (1997), *Facing the Crisis: Selected Texts of Archbishop D.E. Hurley*. Pietermaritzburg: Cluster Publications

Bryan Magee (ed.) (1978), *Men of Ideas: Some Creators of Modern Philosophy*. London: BBC

Smangaliso Mkatshwa (2001), "That Man, Hurley." In: Anthony Gamley (ed.), *Denis Hurley – A Portrait by Friends*. Pietermaritzburg: Cluster Publications, pp. 103-7

Elna Mouton (2008), "Christian Theology at the University: On the threshold or in the margin?" *HTS*, vol. 4, no. 1, pp. 431-45

Peter Randall (ed.) (1982), Not Without Honour: *A Tribute to Beyers Naudé*. Johannesburg: Ravan Press

Colleen Ryan (1990), *Beyers Naudé: Pilgrimage of Faith*. Cape Town: David Philip

Beyers Naudé as Teacher: Memories of a Student

Ben Khumalo-Seegelken

Beyers Naudé was never my teacher; I was never a pupil or a student of his. Beyers Naudé was an elderly friend, an elder brother from whom I learned and I continue to learn to this day. Beyers Naudé has become, yes is my teacher! Mine are, therefore, the reminiscences and remarks of a younger brother – a son – who is learning and is eager to learn more.

Towards the end of my schooldays, between 1968, when I was 17, and 1970, when I was 20, I heard and read for the first time about that Afrikaans-speaking white pastor who for some years already had been targeted and fiercely driven from one controversy to the next by various circles in the leadership of his church, the *Nederduitse Gereformeerde Kerk* (NGK), the Dutch Reformed Church for Afrikaans-speaking Whites. This church was notorious for propagating and practising segregation and subjugation and was home to opinion-leaders in the Afrikaans-speaking white community, including the prime-minister, Verwoerd, and cabinet ministers in the apartheid establishment.

Christiaan Frederick Beyers Naudé had come out and started questioning, preaching about and arguing for the need to do away with apartheid – the need to change! He attracted the attention of many of my age, children and descendants of the local population. Especially the Afrikaans-speaking white community was through its apartheid regime continuing to dispossess this population and had degraded it into a mass of disempowered labourers and voiceless underdogs, whom they collectively called *Nie-Blankes*/Non-Whites or Bantu, *Kleurlinge*/Coloureds, Indians.

Unthinkable encounters

Beyers Naudé started posing those questions our parents and our elder brothers and sisters had been and were asking, and for which many of them were being intimidated or had been silenced. Our questions, our demands were now in the mouth and and the voice of someone "from the other side," who, himself, was still undergoing changes of perception in almost every respect and at high speed. Beyers Naudé was and remained throughout the son of his parents, a member of his Afrikaans-speaking white community, *'n Boer* – as he himself used to say – for life. For all that, however, he became one of the most acknowledged advocates of justice and one of the most impressive examples of a new South African.

We would listen to Beyers Naudé and argue with him as we would debate with an elderly brother, an uncle, a keen teacher, in the days when such encounters between *Blanke*/White and *Nie-Blanke*/Non-White were rare, having been been rendered practically unthinkable by the laws and measures of segregation and subjugation. Some of us in the South African Students' Organisation (SASO) and other groups and organisations within the Black Consciousness Movement (BCM) in those years (1968-72) came to appreciate the exposure to and the confrontation with initiatives and processes connected with Beyers Naudé and the Christian Institute of Southern Africa (CI), of which he was one of the founding members. These initiatives and processes appealed to us more especially because they were direct and frank in their language and authentic in every respect. Some of these initiatives involved ventures into rural areas during school holidays to live with families and assist adults to learn reading and writing. They also involved conversing and exchanging perceptions with them and with local youth on issues and current events in their vicinity and generally (literacy campaigns and awareness workshops).

"Agents of change"

Beyers Naudé had, by then, already been accepted as a reliable advisor and was recognised as a resourceful partner by leaders of congregations and churches that were soon to be referred to as African Independent Churches. Coming into contact with us, Beyers Naudé met equals – certainly no everyday experience for him at all. As daughters and sons of pious believers, most of us had in our early childhood gone through Sunday School, and had gone through the ups and downs of puberty and youth as active members and office bearers in the Student Christian Movement (SCM) in secondary or vocational school and at college. Reading and studying the Bible and arguing about current issues or matters of principle on the basis of our Christian faith constituted the context of social interaction – was the framework of day-to-day communication for most people of my age-group in those days.

I must, however, note that our parents, teachers and local preachers had laid the foundation and made of us budding personalities who could later converse and debate, as we were already starting to do. Among them were the Congregational churchman, Ben Ngidi (*"isikhathi esiphila kusona"*, "the time in which we live"), the Lutheran pastor and theologian, Douglas Makhathini (*"wasiweza ngelibanzi!"*, "and she/he let us all cross over (go free) at ease!") and the Methodist preacher, pathfinder, wise bricklayer, great ecumenical strategist and architect, Enos Sikakane (*"asibhobokelane!"*, "let us break through, relate and exchange perceptions and opinions in genuine openness and mutual trust!").

We youngsters were, however, quite often experienced consternation and indeed indignation when Beyers Naudé would, for example, not avoid sharing platforms with individuals and interest groups who were functionaries and beneficiaries of the apartheid regime – Bantustan functionaries, for example – and were simply unacceptable to us as potential "agents of change". Beyers Naudé exchanged experiences and perceptions with even some of these on "concepts and models of faith in postcolonial Africa" in consultations and workshops held at, among others places, uMphumulo Lutheran Seminary. Beyers Naudé would similarly not hesitate to stand alongside the likes of

Chief Gatsha Buthelezi, head-functionary of the then KwaZulu bantustan, and call for the stopping and withdrawal of investments from South Africa. This was a call we applauded as overdue, a call that, however, could have meant the imposition of the severest sanctions by the apartheid regime on both. Yet it was also a call that revived and enhanced the struggle remarkably, most probably because both Naudé and Buthelezi were so untypical of those in this campaign and so extremely different in their characters and interests, as would become more evident not very long afterwards.

During the years I worked at the Edendale Lay Ecumenical Centre near Pietermaritzburg (1972-75), initiating and coordinating groups of young people mainly in and around Pietermaritzburg and Durban, and facilitating their questioning of and resistance to apartheid, I quite often had to do with Beyers Naudé and others from the CI, which, of course, cooperated with our centre. It was very interesting to observe how polite and correct the encounter and the communication would be. English, a medium that was for us even in those days nobody's own language, enabled us to venture and meet while remaining cautiously aloof. In old age, Beyers Naudé used to smile over one or other phrase – "struggle-vocab" – that used to be typical of certain constellations and levels of communication and debate.

Black consciousness meeting white

Instead of seeking to speak *for* non-Whites, as especially some English-speaking white students and opinion-leaders ("liberals") were occasionally fond of doing in those years, a generation of young white adults had emerged and was taking shape in and around the CI and was focusing on making their own white community aware of and sensitive to the need for change and for cooperating in questioning and challenging apartheid. The walk from Grahamstown to Cape Town, the Pilgrimage of Faith, from 16 December 1972 to mid-January 1973 is one of the initiatives that brought about a conscientisation that was followed by clearer and more adamant ventures in the Struggle – an appealing and a very convincing expression of "White Consciousness."

Three important observations concerning *Oom Bey*, as some of us had in the meantime learned to talk to and about him, come to mind. I shall briefly hint at them, but not go into detail. He was:

- a man fond of stirring quiet waters and of provoking fierce hounds;
- prepared to cooperate possibly always;
- a fieldworker through and through (`n boer – in the best meaning of the word!).

Beyers Naudé could inspire and disappoint interchangeably and continually, but one would be keen to rely on him all the same. Three instances come to mind. I refer to them in brief:

- The Special Fund of the WCC Programme to Combat Racism. Initially, Beyers Naudé responded in contradictory terms and disappointed many of us in our unconditional approval of the Special Fund as an expression of genuine solidarity with the liberation struggle.

• A pastor preaching about "Obedience to God" in the face of a Commission of Inquiry into certain Organisations (the Schlebusch-Commission). He used this theme to substantiate his decision to refuse in protest to testify before the Commission (1973), thereby laying ground for and giving a comprehensive theological argument for "civil disobedience as divine obedience," an argument that inspired many of us enormously!

• Annual Conference of the South African Council of Churches (SACC) at Hammanskraal in 1975. Especially notable were his arguments in favour of a resolution calling for conscientious objection to compulsory military conscription and highlighting the need for chaplaincy to armed units of the liberation movement in exile and underground. His was a truly prophetic voice!

Photo: Lasse Herneklint

Johannesburg 1984. Beyers Naudé in conversation with two women after morning service.

Much later – 1985 – meeting in exile

Ilse and Beyers Naudé participated in a conference in Arnoldshain (Germany) in which many exiled South Africans took part. As everybody was about leave at the end of the weekend, my elder son (8), who had been playing amusedly with Ilse and Beyers now and again during the conference, asked: "Papa, how do I say in their language: 'Kommt uns bald in Düsseldorf besuchen!' (Come and visit us soon in Düsseldorf!)?" You won't believe it, but that simple sentence was no longer so easy for me to translate into Afrikaans! I suddenly realised how much of a language I had learned at school up to university, and that commanded almost as much as any other had faded from my cognitive memory since I had started resisting apartheid conscientiously. Afrikaans, the language of the oppressor, had since then not crossed my lips and I had simply wiped it from my mind.

The desire of my little boy in 1985 to remain in contact with the old folks he had just met, made me instantly realise that people engaged in resisting and fighting apartheid included Ilse and Beyers Naudé, Allan Boesak, David Bosch and many others who were living and striving in the first place in their mother tongue, Afrikaans. This is what Ilse and Beyers had always done and were doing, apparently such that my own son responded to them as naturally as he did!

That get together in Arnoldshain in 1985 made me realise even more clearly that overcoming apartheid entailed liberating Afrikaans and other languages from the role the apartheid system had assigned them as vehicles and instruments of segregation and subjugation. The future beyond apartheid was one in which everyone would in every respect live on par with everybody else. Oom Bey and I could then affirm: Fighting against apartheid in Zulu, Afrikaans, Xhosa, Tswana, Sotho, means fighting for a future in which people will live together in freedom – conversing, celebrating and hoping in Zulu, Afrikaans, Xhosa, Tswana, Sotho!

Since 1994

In my meetings since 1994 with Ilse and Beyers Naudé at their home and later in the old age home in Johannesburg, we would look back and chat. Once, after the inauguration of the Beyers Naudé Drive in Johannesburg, Oom Bey, seemingly overwhelmed, remarked: "Did anyone of us ever really hope to live long enough to witness the days in which the change we envisaged finally starts coming about?"

I keep on asking to this day: What did I learn? What do I learn?

A Response to Ben Khumalo-Seegelken

Hans S.A. Engdahl

It is a pleasure reading Ben Khumalo-Seegelken's text about Beyers Naudé. There is a closeness and yet respect for the person Beyers Naudé, a real *Boer*. What adds value to Khumalo-Seegelken's paper is that he is part of this very history and has continued to be so since migrating to Europe. I can only agree with the main thrust of his paper.

My own encounters with Beyers Naudé come much later, from the mid-1980s onwards. We met at the World Council of Churches in Geneva and on a regular basis in Stockholm and Uppsala. At this time (1987-90), I was refused a visa by South Africa, so having Beyers Naudé visit us in Sweden was a way of keeping in close touch with events. He was much in demand in those days: church, government and media – all opened their doors to him. What one remembers from his press conferences, often held at the foreign office at Fredsgatan, Stockholm, was his absolute concentration, no manuscript, always speaking to the point. What he served the information-hungry media was always some kind of résumé of the (political) state of affairs in South Africa. Very few could at the time do this kind of thing, but a representative of the church like him could.

Uppsala 1991. Beyers Naudé and Hans S.A. Engdahl. In the background, Uppsala Cathedral.

A major point in Khumalo-Seegelken's paper regards the relationship between the Black Consciousness Movement and Beyers Naudé and others at the Christian Institute. This is indeed a crucial aspect of Naudé's ministry, which has often been ignored.

Those who have read anything about Steve Biko, the founder of Black Consciousness, would know that the student body NUSAS (National Union of South African Students) played an important role as a catalyst in formulating and forming Black Consciousness. This liberal body seemed to have all the right opinions, but did not appreciate the need for stressing blackness in any sense of the word. The net result in the 1970s was a supposedly non-racial student movement firmly in the hands of whites.

A "beyond" in this struggle

What I want to address is the question why Beyers Naudé could understand Black Consciousness while NUSAS possibly could not. In confronting the British Empire,

Naudé and his Afrikaner people had had an experience that was similar to that of the blacks. At one point, Steve Biko met with Afrikaner students in Cape Town. Biko commented:

> When I addressed a group in Cape Town ... I spoke about our viewpoint, and incidentally this was found most acceptable by the Afrikaner students. They said to me in no uncertain terms: This is the way Afrikaner nationalism developed, right; we wish you guys well ... [Johan Fick, president of the Afrikaner Studentebond] recognized what I was saying as what had been said in his history (cited in Engdahl 2012: 22).

To a degree, it was the same struggle that had to be fought, a struggle that Naudé knew well from his Afrikaner forebears (he was named after General Beyers, who had fought against the British colonialists). The task was to "build up a new consciousness that would eventually help people come into their own, on an individual as well as on a collective basis" (cited in Engdahl 2012: 22).

Khumalo-Seegelken does not mention it, but there may have been an inherent weakness in this kind of shared ground, and the liberals may have had a point. There should be a "beyond" in this struggle, there must come a day when Afrikanerdom and Black Consciousness are transformed into something greater, something more comprehensive. The current debate in South Africa is exactly about this issue. Some believe, and I am among them, that Biko envisaged something beyond what was at stake in the apartheid era, and yet, he would have held true to the very same concept as long as blacks continued to belong to the underclass, to be discriminated against, as in today's South Africa.

After 32 years of absence

"Faith as Politics," the theme of the publication, is a very apt caption for the life of Beyers Naudé. One could say that his life world of Reformed theology had an almost direct bearing on political realities. It is therefore no wonder that his life forms a trajectory that has such an immediate and consistent bearing on the fate of South Africa. His threefold conversion is made manifest in three sermons: the first saying that the cross of Christ was everything (1 Corinthians 2.2); the second, on his parting of ways from the Dutch Reformed Church for the Christian Institute, declaring that "you must obey God rather than men" (Acts 5.9); and the third being the actual decision to openly confront the apartheid state ("Is not my word ... says the Lord, ... like a hammer that breaks a rock in pieces?" Jeremia 23.29). There is also his remarkable *deursettingsvermoë* (persistence and consistence); his utter humility in saying "as an Afrikaner you are nothing," yet his pride in stating that he is one; the role of his wife Ilse, who brought the whole ethos of the Moravian mission into their relationship (with an open door to change and integration); his theology, which had to be made real in practice rather than in theory.

It has been said that Beyers Naudé's life had come full circle when in 1995, after 32 years of absence, he was welcomed back to his old congregation in the Dutch Reformed Church at Aasvoëlkop in Pretoria. He preached on the theme 'n *Pleidooi vir versoening* (A plea for reconciliation). This sermon bears witness to his greatness. Softly he talks about the task of the Christian to work towards reconciliation at all costs. He also mentions the question of guilt, i.e., the obligation of restitution (issues of land, properties, etc.), but he does it in such a way so as to include himself. He asks for forgiveness in case he has given offence to anybody through his actions.

The dire need for economic justice

I am not certain that his life came full circle here. What we witnessed at Aasvoëlkop was a personal return to an environment from which he had been banned for so many years. But make no mistake (a favourite expression of his), his life had not come to a close. There was much more to be done. The struggle had to continue. The sad part of this reconciliatory venture is that it could easily be used by whites as proof that things were now in order: justice has been done, and we can rest on our laurels. Not so: Beyers Naudé was fully aware of the blatant injustices that were still there. One of the most obvious facts, staring you in the face, was the abject poverty that blacks still found themselves in.

In the 1990s, Beyers Naudé was instrumental in setting up a task force within the South African Council of Churches to deal with economic injustice, the Ecumenical Service for Socio Economic Transformation (ESSET). It was a radical programme, and assumed that any democratically elected government had direct responsibility for the plight of the poor in a country that was rich in resources.

My conviction is that had Beyers Naudé been actively involved with us in 2015, he would have emphasised, above all else, the dire need for economic justice. And he would speak out against corruption in all places, not least in high places. He would not only speak, he would, if he were still able, be deeply involved in various action groups. We have not yet come full circle. Thanks to people like Beyers Naudé, we realise that this struggle must go on, seemingly without end.

References

Steve Biko (1978), *Black Consciousness in South Africa*. Edited by Millard W Arnold. New York: Random House

Hans Engdahl (2012), "Theology as Politics in Afrikaner Nationalism and Black Consciousness. A Close Reading of F.J.M. Potgieter and Steve Biko," *Journal of Theology for Southern Africa*, vol. 144, November, pp. 4-25

Mark Sanders (2002), *Complicities: The Intellectual and Apartheid*. Durham, NC and London: Duke University Press

Beyers Naudé's Prophetic Voice: More than a time-piece to remind us of the horrors of apartheid

Horst Kleinschmidt

On the anniversary of his 100th birthday, Beyers Naudé is being honoured in Uppsala, Stellenbosch, Cape Town, Durban, Alexandra outside Johannesburg, UNISA in Pretoria and in other places. Beyers Naudé's quest for *egalité* was fundamental and applies today as it did under apartheid. It applies in South Africa as it applies elsewhere in the world.

Maya Angelou, the American writer, has said, "History, despite its wrenching pain cannot be unlived. But, if faced with courage, need not be lived again".[1] These are compelling words. She calls on us to remember, but equally to stand vigilant lest what happened before happens again.

Howard Zinn, historian, playwright and author wrote: "The future is an infinite succession of presents, and to live now as we think human beings should live, in defiance of all that is bad around us, is itself a marvelous victory".[2]

I chose these quotations because they evoke different yet complementary aspects of *Oom Bey*, and why his life warrants our attention. Beyers not only helped lead us out of apartheid, his prophecy includes a demand for a just and equal society, and *as part of his quest for egalité* he shunned a lavish lifestyle – yes, even accepted insecurity in solidarity with others. If Beyers was with us today, he would still be driving a lovingly and personally serviced 50-year-old Peugeot 404 to get to meetings against xenophobia in informal settlements, while at the same time supporting those campaigning for land, housing and sanitation.

Detaching from the poor at lightning speed

Slowly, very slowly, it is dawning on collective South Africa that the right to cast our vote since 1994 has not resulted in all we had hoped for and expected. Nineteen ninety-four did provide significant gains for those who most needed freedom from the racial dispensation of apartheid, but it continues to leave the majority

- without a better education,
- desperate and in grinding poverty,

---

[1] Maya Angelou Black History Month Special 'Telling Our Stories' Celebrates Past And Present (huffingtonpost.com, 20 February 2013)
[2] Howard Zinn quotes at goodreads.com, www.goodreads.com/author/quotes/1899.Howard_Zinn

- and handicapped by systemic inequality.

To throw off the yoke of apartheid was momentous and required an arduous struggle with enormous sacrifices. Let us always be thankful that the advent of democracy has outlawed racist conduct, and has given us an exceptional constitution, an independent judiciary and a Bill of Rights to be proud of.

However, the transformation project remains substantially deficient and unfulfilled. This is because of failings by those who promised change in the name of revolution. Their poor decisions, their vulgar indulgence in wining and dining (politicians and civil servants alike), their attachment to ostentation and lavish fashion shows in parliament and unacceptably glitzy cars, and now the rise of a new bigotry within their own ranks, combine to threaten the gains of 1994. Our current rulers have it in them to take us into a new darkness – and I don't mean the darkness caused by our power utility, Eskom. The ANC's detachment from the poor happened at lightning speed. We are now at the bottom of the inequality rankings globally.

We have a problem! The new political elite is in a tight embrace with the old white moneyed elite, which in turn is in cosy cahoots with a sprinkling of indebted black capitalists. They are stunningly unconcerned about the plight of the poor and rely, as in the apartheid era, on the police to quell unrest rather than on politicians to deal with its causes. Unrest, as yet uncoordinated, now erupts somewhere in South Africa every single day. At times, our highways, the arteries between major towns, have been disrupted and traffic prevented from passing. In suppressing the revolt, the guarantees in our Bill of Rights are already being regularly violated. We may indeed anticipate states of emergency, like those under apartheid. I believe that it is not premature to ask whether this massive political failure opens the gates for a Julius Malema, leader of the Economic Freedom Fighters, to become the authoritarian head of state, not to say *Führer*. His propensity for racial slurs is already used to serve his personal and his political ends.

Smuggled letters

Where would Beyers Naudé be in all of this if he were with us today?

Allow me to explain: *Oom Bey* was out of sight from 1977 until his house arrest (banning) was lifted in 1984. But he did not sit and do nothing. In those seven long years, Beyers's prophetic witness was infused with radical new thoughts and action, taking his ever deeply held Christian belief into the politics of the day. For him, there was no contradiction. The history I highlight below, I believe, leaves his integrity intact and his stature all the greater.

The thread throughout is that Beyers implores us never to drop the baton 1) for the defence of our fundamental rights and 2) for true equality. In a letter smuggled out of the country and dated 27 October 1977, a week after the Christian Institute (CI), as well as all the staff, including Beyers, were banned, he wrote:

> As I have indicated … I'm willing to serve wherever my presence could make the greatest and most meaningful contribution. In view of the situation created by the recent events it seems to me to be clear that for the foreseeable future my task is to remain where I am but we are considering this situation as well as the implications of staying or leaving and we shall keep you informed.

A few weeks later – in late 1977 – Beyers briefly, but seriously, considered leaving South Africa to make common cause in exile in Lusaka with Oliver Tambo and the ANC, and with Mangosutho Buthelezi. The idea was to break the stalemate that apartheid had brought about in Southern Africa. But a year later, in a letter dated 9 October 1978, Beyers wrote:

> My future position and role: I want to make it quite clear that as long as God gives me the necessary mental and physical strength, I shall continue with the work of the CI. I have no intention of withdrawing or "retiring" or discarding the task in which I am involved. This is how I see my position here in SA and, however difficult it may be, I hope to continue to provide the leadership here in our country with the full awareness that a moment may arrive where I may find it impossible to continue – but if and when that moment comes, I shall clearly say so and share my position with the group.

These smuggled letters, and many more in his distinctive handwriting, are still in my possession.

In the early months of 1978, Beyers and the "group" (insiders, mostly former CI staff members) were involved in drawing up a policy paper, the intent of which was to build a framework and role for an illegal, underground CI. The document addresses:

Some pages from one of many smuggled letters of Beyers Naudé, written during his banning. In this one, dated 30 April 1983, he seeks funding for the Congress of South African Students.

- how and on what basis to work with the exiled ANC, the Black Consciousness Movement and possibly with Inkatha;
- the role and task of individual Christians and of the churches in South Africa;
- the need to provide on-the-spot analyses of the South African situation as a tool to challenge the churches' ambivalent stand towards apartheid, inside South Africa and in Europe and North America;
- promoting reconciliation and unity between "liberation groups,"
- providing pastoral care to exiles and training opportunities for those apartheid was failing;
- establishing a "Steve Biko Institute;"
- ways in which an underground CI might support internal popular mobilisation;
- cooperation with the OAU and the UN; and
- ways to upscale non-violent struggle, without seeking to replace the armed struggle pursued by the ANC and PAC.

Although such a structure failed to materialise, Beyers and his inner circle pursued these objectives during his eight-year banning order.

As uncomfortable as yesterday

As is known, Beyers was invited to the first *Groote Schuur* talks as a negotiator on the side of the ANC. However, he was not seen in subsequent negotiations. Was he dropped because his moral Christian socialism did not fit into the modalities of what the parties to our new dispensation had in mind? I don't know the answer to this question. Even when he was confined to a wheelchair, he warned against the ease with which the new ruling party immersed itself in comfort and luxury, and then sank into corruption on an unprecedented scale. As could be expected of him, Beyers was already a step ahead and could not be part of the compromises the incoming order made.

GROOTE SCHUUR in Cape Town was the official prime minister residence and the site for the negotiations between the African National Congress and the Apartheid Regime.

In another initiative that involved both him and his wife Ilse, they raised very considerable financial resources to change the Dutch Reformed Church from within. Through their travel and exposure to ecumenical developments in Europe, Beyers and Ilse had changed their outlook, their *Weltanschauung*. They now wanted to expose others to a similar experience. Later this year, I anticipate we will see a new publication that details how Ilse and Beyers quietly ran the Christian Fellowship Trust.[3] From 1965 to 1995, for 30 years, they sent over 400 persons overseas to experience what they themselves had experienced. It was Beyers's intention to change the Dutch Reformed Church in this way.

---

[3] The University of Free State Press is currently considering a manuscript submitted to them.

The above narrative lifts the lid, ever so slightly, on the secret, the subversive, political, but deeply Christian Beyers Naudé. Beyers should be celebrated for all of what he was and did. We must allow no one to sanitise Beyers. To honour Oom Bey, he needs to be as uncomfortable in our consciences today as he was yesterday.

Beyers's roots in the struggle for Afrikaner economic rights in the face of British imperial dominance left him knowing the concept of class. From 1977 on, Beyers spoke, wrote and sought to better understand the system of exploitation of one class by another. He wrestled to understand and connect the ideology of Black Consciousness and its uneasy relationship with class. All of this thinking led him to seek economic equality in a political order that did not accept and then compound the distortions capitalism has created and continues to create. He was not content merely to oppose corruption and authoritarian trends before and after 1994. In my view, Beyers may indeed be remembered as a Christian socialist, as a humanitarian socialist.

Beyers's respect for and recognition of every single individual, irrespective of his or her station in life, is well known, and so is his far-sightedness. But there is another side of Beyers that warrants attention. It is his concern and care for the wrongdoer. He condemned no one and went to incredible lengths to redeem those condemned for whatever reason. Beyers knew ostracism. He spoke with pain about his Christmas holidays in Onrust, Southern Cape, when his morning walk to buy the Afrikaans and English newspapers felt like running the gauntlet. For historic reasons, a number of top Afrikaner leaders spent their holidays in the same village. Even though they had known Beyers from the time before he broke ranks, they ignored him.[4]

I want to take Beyers's concern for the ostracised to another level. Those who voted for apartheid, those whom the white English, but not them alone, conveniently and gratuitously refer to as "those Afrikaners" are still today, in many, many instances considered near pariahs. The term Afrikaner or Boer is so very often used in a loaded way. The antipathy towards apartheid's proponents may have some justification, but I think Beyers would want to reach out to them. I have always felt it scandalous how the last apartheid president, F.W. de Klerk, and his elite group walked away from their most loyal constituency, taking none of the blame. Much worse, de Klerk et al. made next to no effort to re-educate their people and lead them out of the darkness the National Party had moulded for them. It cannot be right that we leave tens of thousands of apartheid adherents to smoulder in isolation, with next to no effort being made to redeem them from their own past. Nation-building cannot happen when one section of our people is consigned to a ghetto through finger pointing. Somehow, it is assumed they should discover for themselves how to be liberated. I submit that Beyers would not have been blind to this aspect of the incomplete transition we are in today. Beyers would not be seen among the legions of victors who through the ages have self-righteously pointed accusing fingers at "them".

---

[4] Much later, when these same politicians considered negotiations and talks with the ANC, Beyers recalled that these individuals who used to ignore him now stopped him in the shop in Onrust at Christmas time and said: *"Beyers, ons moet praat!"* (Beyers, we need to talk).

Horst Kleinschmidt and his wife at the time, Ilona Aronson, were active, together with Beyers Naudé, in the anti-apartheid struggle already in the early 1970s. They were closely surveyed by the security branch and the Schlebusch Commission, established in 1972 by the South African government to investigate anti-apartheid civil society organizations.

In an unpublished interview, Beyers, true to character, asks: "What is there that I can do to share in building a new and just society?" These are his words spoken not prior to 1994, but just before the year 2000. Beyers's quest for *egalité* has not been remotely achieved. I urge you to honour him appropriately. Guard against a memory of Beyers that is an annual ritual which leaves a warm and fuzzy feeling about a hero of the past. Beyers would not want to be made into a static monument. Beyers's life is an inspiration to us to never drop the baton in the struggle for equality.

Johannesburg 1985. Birgitta Karlström Dorph and Beyers Naudé in the garden at Beyers' daughter Liesel's home, a place where they often met.

A Response to Horst Kleinschmidt

Birgitta Karlström Dorph

What an honour, Beyers, to take part in the celebration of your 100 years. You are still very much alive in many people's minds. To me personally, it all seems so near and at the same time so very far away. Before I comment on Horst's thoughts, and the Swedish support for the apartheid resistance inside South Africa, I will, if you will allow me, be personal and share a sweet memory of you. You were here in Sweden on your 70th birthday, in 1985. I had just had my youngest daughter. You called me in the hospital. I told you that I wanted to give her the name Beyers. That, I think, is the only time you fell very quiet.

Our first meeting

I was working with the Swedish Legation in Pretoria during the 1980s, one of the most critical and violent times in the struggle. It was a time when everything was building up towards the end, the end of apartheid and victory. As resistance became more active, repression intensified and confrontation sharpened. My assignment was twofold: to extend support inside the country to the resistance and to follow what was happening in the country. This was an unusual task. We were the representatives of the government of Prime Minister Palme to the government of President Botha. At the same time, we were supposed to support resistance inside the country with Swedish government funds. It was tricky, like walking on a knife's edge. Political analysis was important and personal contacts were vital. How to build them up?

I saw you Beyers regularly, more or less every week for an hour or two, during all those years. I actually met you my very first week in South Africa. I remember how nervous I was to meet this icon for the first time. I was late, it was not easy to find the road. You quickly made me feel at ease, there was some magic in your way with people. I followed you through the political and social developments during the 1980s. We used to meet in your daughter's house. I went there along various roads and always brought some buns, we made tea together and would then sit outside in the garden, so that it would be more difficult for outsiders to eavesdrop – listening devices were always suspected. You were banned when we first met.

A new wave of resistance – early 1980s

During those years, with your sharp brain, you held up a mirror for me on what was happening in South Africa; you gave me your views and ideas; you informed me about developments and organisations; you analysed the activities of the government and of the resistance; you told me about how your unbanning was announced and described in a funny way how the police were marching towards your house. We discussed the state of emergency, restrictions on travel, the fundraising act, funerals, bannings, political trials, the security police, yes just about everything concerning South African developments. You were thinking aloud about taking on the task of secretary general of the South African Council of Church. I also attended your first sermon in a church in Pretoria after your unbanning. I visited you after I had left South Africa. Once I got stuck on Beyers Naudé Drive, the old Malan Drive. You laughed and said: "That is the way they honour us, Birgitta."

Without you, we on the Swedish side would never have achieved what we did. Especially in the beginning, I would have been totally lost without you. The situation was complicated because we in Sweden did not have thorough information about developments in South Africa. This was a result of our boycotts and bans. Very few Swedes came to South Africa and virtually nobody in the resistance travelled from South Africa to Sweden. Of course, we had information through political refugees and in many other ways, not least the churches, but still day-to-day first-hand information was important. Slowly, I was able to build up more knowledge and a trusted circle of contacts, actually friends.

I travelled around with Elias, a wonderful driver, looked up people and visited organisations, talked, but above all listened. You helped a lot by building confidence and trust. Trust was the keyword: without trust on both sides nothing could be done. For me, it was of utmost importance to meet people in their own environments in order to understand what was needed, what they wanted and where we from the Swedish side could fit in. A new wave of resistance was arising at the beginning of the 1980s. New organisations were being born all over, trade unions, civics, youth, women.

No conditional ties

Who and what could we support? Our support was built up and extended to a range of organisations – some not very controversial and quite open in order to be able to support other, more militant organisations. We wanted to bring humanitarian assistance and relief to the oppressed people, so that they could participate in bringing about fundamental change. In one sense, the work became easier with time because I got to know and understand more, but from a security point of view it became more and more difficult for the resistance to operate. Constant changes had to be made. It also became more difficult to transfer money. The fundraising act was tightened. We tried to be as legal as possible, as we did not want to be pushed out. We did not want the authorities to close the legation or declare me *persona non grata*. Then, our work would become much more difficult.

It was not the Swedish government that was working with the organisations in South Africa. It was the whole Swedish family of NGOs and also political organisations, trade unions and churches. They became partners with the organisations in South Africa. The Swedish groups received money from the Swedish government and then in various ways it was sent to South Africa. Sweden came to fund many different projects involving the resistance in all parts of society. Actually, we became part of funding a new civil society. The family of organisations we supported became more multifaceted. Civics, legal organisations, advocates, trade unions, churches, health clinics, education, students, scholarships, street organisations, townships, youth, women, media, publishing companies, the arts, small clubs, and the umbrella United Democratic Front organisation. Our support expanded very rapidly. Of course, the organisations did not want to be dependent on outside funding. On our side, we had no conditional ties whatsoever. I think we came to support at least 400 organisations. Most of them we started work with through my initiatives and my visits to them. Up until we started cooperation with them, many of them were unknown in Sweden. You were vital in that connection.

Horst – some kind of magician

Many hundreds of million Swedish Kronor went to the resistance inside the country – nobody has yet calculated how much altogether. Our support for the external ANC was well known. We were by far the biggest supporter in the Western world. But our support inside the country became much bigger and is still largely unknown, partly because it was so secret. Many people witnessed how important the support became in the struggle. During all those years, you Beyers shared your knowledge and wisdom. Problems often occurred, difficult questions came up regularly. I always went back to you when I needed advice or was hesitant. Should we support a particular project? What did things really mean? Sometimes you said you wanted to think about something or consult others to find out.

You came back to me with answers to difficult issues, answers that made a lot of sense, answers which were grounded in the resistance and which were workable. During your banned years, I think you in a way had more time for reflection and more time to see all sorts of people. Actually I felt that I was part of a large circle of South African disciples who came to you to discuss and listen. You had a strict schedule. Many of the future leaders were groomed by you during those years. Even now when I listen to certain people, I can feel that it is you who speak through them, not only in terms of what they say, but also how they say it. Clear, distinctive and with a way to explain complicated matters so they become easier to understand. I remember how we were sitting under a tree, I with my notebook you with your depth of knowledge and twinkle in your eyes. You often said I will see what Horst can do about that. It was many years before I met him, I did not know who this Horst was, but I understood that he was some kind of magician. That I one day would be in Uppsala talking to him about you, I could never have imagined. It is a magic moment in my life.

In your spirit, we should continue

When I think of you Beyers, I think of wisdom, knowledge, patience, trust, humour, of very special moments. Horst has said it all so well today. The thread throughout is that you implore us never to drop the baton of struggle in the defence of fundamental rights and for true equality. You would have fought for that. South Africa should rise from its present bottom ranking when it comes to global inequality, as Horst is emphasising. Rebels like you are not just born, they flourish when the environment nurtures them. You showed respect and recognition for every single individual, and concern for the wrongdoer.

I wonder what you would have said about the new darkness Horst speaks of, and the plight of the poor. I hear what Horst says about the inaction of de Klerk and his friends by walking away from their most loyal constituency with nearly no effort being made for them to be redeemed from their own past. You would not have been blind to that. There are other aspects of you, that Horst touched upon – for example, your subversiveness. Much more should be said about that when the time comes. And last but always not least, your tremendous sense of humour Beyers, which broke through many things, even when the issues and days were tough. You should, as Horst says, be celebrated for all that your were and did.

Horst has said that a prophet speaks of the possibilities and dangers that face us not tomorrow, but the day after tomorrow. Beyers, you have given us the inspiration to work for a better world. In your spirit, we should continue.

Cottesloe, Johannesburg, December 1960. Beyers Naudé with Reverends Sidebothan and Webb.

Beyers Naudé and the Theology of Reconciliation

Christo Lombard

I have been asked to address the topic, as given above, in my contribution to the centenary celebrations of Beyers Naudé's life and work. Initially, I wondered why this focus on "reconciliation" was chosen, since my own thinking has been influenced, from the early days of my studies in philosophy in the mid-1960s, more specifically by what I always viewed as his heroic work for justice and truth. As a young student, I had the privilege of meeting this friendly and approachable Afrikaner prophet several times at clandestine meetings of small Christian Institute (CI) cells in Stellenbosch. Also, at later meetings (for instance, when he spoke on the prophetic role of the church in Windhoek),[1] his warm and reconciling presence impressed me. In spite of his charming and outgoing personality, my own association with his legacy has always been geared more towards "justice issues" than "reconciliation." However, when I started reading Beyers Naudé's work again, in preparation for this short chapter, I was struck and pleasantly surprised by the centrality of the concept and reality of reconciliation

---

[1] This was in the 1980s, when I was involved in the Department of Religion and Theology at the University of Namibia.

"And he died for all, that those who live should no longer live for themselves but for him who died for them and was raised again"

– 2 Corinthians 5:15

in his life and work. I can now say with conviction that for him these two, justice and reconciliation, are two sides of the same coin, and they cannot be separated or played off against one another.

I shall try to make this point by approaching our topic via a few selected texts and events from Beyers Naudé's life and work, jumping – as it were – from the one to the other. I do this, however, within a historical framework that identifies the major "chapters" in the development of his theology. I thus try to follow the logic of his developing thinking from different phases in his own "ministry of reconciliation." Two texts will serve as anchors and will be dealt with in more detail: an early document (from 1963) in which he spells out his vision of reconciliation for the work of the CI, and a rather late sermon from 1995, at Aasvoëlkop, when he completed the circle by again preaching on reconciliation and, in fact, reconciling with the congregation he had had to leave 32 years earlier to start the CI. It will hopefully be shown that these two key documents are linked, and shadowed by several similar texts from the more than three decades that separate them.[2]

The argument presented here has four major elements: we start with a key text on reconciliation (1); then we trace the influences from Beyers Naudé's youth and formative years on his theological thinking (2); before investigating a few selected texts from each of the phases of his theological development, illustrating his evolving thinking on reconciliation (3); while ending with a final, "vindicating" text on reconciliation (4), hopefully also bringing the argument full circle.

A key text on reconciliation

A key text that clearly illustrates the connection between justice and reconciliation in Beyers Naudé's thinking is his sermon from 1963 on 2 Cor 5:15-21, Paul's classic text dealing with "the ministry of reconciliation." It is certainly meaningful that Bey-

---

[2] "Similar," in that these texts illustrate the centrality of reconciliation, while always linking it with justice. It is not possible to include all the relevant texts from Beyers Naudé's vast bibliography, as, for example, his many *Pro Veritate* contributions. Here I concentrate on the literature brought together, more recently, in accessible format by the Beyers Naudé Centre for Public Theology, and one or two other standard books on his life and work.

ers Naudé spoke about exactly this ministry on the occasion when he accepted the directorship of the CI. This text shows clearly that while he worked for justice against oppression, apartheid and poverty, the heart of his ministry was one of *obedience* to God alone, and *truthfulness*. It was nothing other than a ministry of *reconciliation*, based on God's forgiveness and grace, which the church as the body of Christ, and every Christian individually, had to emulate and incarnate in obedience and truthfulness.

On 15 December 1963, Beyers Naudé took upon himself the directorship of the newly formed CI and on that occasion, at the Methodist Central Hall in Johannesburg, he spoke on the practical demands and implications of reconciliation. He started by saying:

> I have chosen as the theme the concept of reconciliation as in 2 Cor. 5:14-21 because of reasons which may be obvious to some of you but which, I hope, will become quite clear to all of you as we proceed. Let us for a moment give our attention to the term. Not only is *reconciliation* a biblical term but it is quite clearly a biblical truth – a New Testament concept which we should grasp and apply in honesty and humility if we want to call ourselves Christians. This is a wholly-Christian concept, because the world knows and understands nothing about reconciliation. The world knows about compromise and concession, yes, and appeasement and adaptation, but reconciliation is a totally new concept, which only the New Testament has proclaimed because it means in essence the supreme act of sacrificial love of God to restore the true relation between God and man, and between man and man.[3]

Naudé then asks, "What does this imply?" ("this" meaning the centrality, for Christian faith and the church, of the truth of reconciliation). He answers by mentioning four implications, asking a telling rhetorical question at the end of each, which will be fully quoted here.

The first implication is that God, to "man's" amazement, is calling "him" to a new understanding, attitude and acceptance of God's *forgiveness*, as preached and practised by Christ: without willingness to forgive all truly and fully, no reconciliation is possible. To drive home the point, he then asks: "Do we realise the challenge this holds for us as Christians, that as long as we harbour a spirit of unforgiveness in our hearts, any reconciliation is made impossible? That we are, in fact, thwarting the purpose and the will of God?"[4]

The second implication is that God's offer of reconciliation was not made to the church as such, or to Christians as a separate group, but it was made to *the world* – the world in its lostness; to people and nations in their hatred, selfishness, waywardness and bitterness: this is the "world" which God had reconciled to God-self. "Do we reali-

---

[3] Hansen 2005: 139
[4] All four questions, following here, come from Hansen (2005: 140). This text in many ways speaks along similar lines, and in the same spirit, as the much later Belhar Confession, which also identified the assumption of "irreconcilability" in apartheid thinking as the heart of the matter, indeed as blasphemy and heresy.

se the direct challenge this one word, *world*, in 2 Cor. 5:19 brings to us? How far does our world go? Do we include – and exclude – in our love and fellowship those whom God includes and excludes? Or do we build up our own walls and barriers contrary to God's command?"

The third implication of God's reconciliation is that it was not meant only as a verbal message but as an incarnated reality, as shown by Christ's willingness to "pay the price" with his own life. "Do we realise that our confession of faith becomes nothing but cheap talk, yes, becomes an act of hypocrisy if we do not fully accept and enact the reconciliation of God in our lives?"

The fourth implication of New Testament reconciliation is that God's reconciliation with us has direct consequences for our relations as humans – "man to man." All human relations are thereby affected and transformed: by a new quality, content, spirit and approach that goes against any sinful division, misunderstanding, animosity, prejudice or fear that taint our relations. Christians who live by God's forgiveness and reconciliation must do everything in their power through words and acts of love, through persistent prayers, to illustrate the truth of reconciliation in all their relations.

> Do we as Christians realise and accept this as an individual moral obligation which we dare not shirk whether our church assist us or not? But do we also realise that, as God's reconciliation has gone out to the world, our witness must also become an outreach to non-Christians, to all who stand aloof, who are critical or hostile towards Christianity and the Church? [5]

Having spelt out the implications of reconciliation in the context in which the new CI was launched, Naudé addresses the further question: "How do we implement this? Where do we start and how far do we go?" His answer is, short and sweet: that there is no reconciliation possible without *conversation* and *communication* and that our starting point will and always must be Christ our Lord – his word, his spirit, his example, his life. "The moment we acknowledge this, a central unity of conviction replaces all our lesser loyalties, all our minor differences of culture, politics or race".[6] Stressing the latent goodwill among Afrikaans- and English-speaking, and white and "non-white" Christians in South Africa, he addresses the need for "a broad concept of unity, of common sacrifice and service from all sections to all sections of our multi-cultural and multi-racial country",[7] which will only become a reality when our prejudices, fears and hatreds are broken down and new trust built in and through Jesus Christ.[8]

Finally, he stressed the urgency of this "ministry of reconciliation" in South Africa,

---

[5] Hansen 2005:140.
[6] Hansen 2005: 141.
[7] Hansen 2005: 141
[8] One cannot help but think of the language of the much later Belhar Confession: the church's task is to foster the unity, reconciliation and the justice of God's kingdom in the world.

to which he committed the CI by, interestingly enough, addressing the consequences if closer Christian fellowship and the better understanding that could come out of improved communication did *not* materialise; if these tools of reconciliation were continually discouraged, criticised, scoffed and rejected "through an increased process of isolation or secret machinations":

> Where there is little or no communication through contact and consultation on the basis of love and truth, there is no possibility of true communion of mind and spirit. And where true communion is lacking or ailing, a false communion based on a false brotherhood, for example communism, takes over. Therefore, the only adequate answer to all forms and possible growth of communism is for Christians to create a communion and a community of love, mutual understanding and respect … That is why the final answer to the communist must be the fullness of life and love which only Christ can give.[9]

Committing the CI as an added channel, an instrument of conversation, consultation, even consecration, for Christian groups of all backgrounds to come together, to share their faith and fears, to communicate with one another about the things of the kingdom, to experience deeper fellowship, Beyers Naudé concludes this programmatic vision of reconciliation for South Africa as follows:

> Only in and through Christ and his reconciling work can we hope to attain the leadership which God expects of his followers in this crucial hour of our history. But this will only be achieved if we first rediscover our unity in Christ, reaffirming our faith in Him as Lord, and rededicate ourselves for every sacrifice which He demands. Then, and only then, will we as Christians be able to give a witness which through its spiritual and moral strength, will transform the hearts of men and change the destiny of our country. Christians of South Africa let us hear and obey! [10]

While this theology remained the constant mainstay of his theological praxis, even when different nuances were given in different contexts, it is worthwhile studying the development of his *application*, over many years, of this line of the Scottish evangelical-reformed theology in which he was brought up.[11]

We shall now first trace some formative events from Beyers Naudé's youth and early adult life that helped to shape his theology, specifically his thinking about reconciliation, before focusing on the different contexts in which he applied this theology.

---

[9] Hansen 2005: 141-2. How ironic that a person offering such a clear "answer" to the problem of radical forces that might take over if the way of the gospel is not followed, would himself be accused of being a "communist"!

[10] Hansen 2005: 142

[11] This theological line has recently become the focus of serious studies that demarcate it from other influential lines, such as the Neo-Calvinist and the Neo-Fichtian romantic nationalist lines, in different "stages" of his theological development. See Durand (in Villa-Vicencio and De Gruchy 1985: 39-51); also Brümmer 2013).

The Broederbond, a Freemason-like society for Afrikaner nationalists, was founded in 1918 under the name Jong Zuid Afrika, 'Young South Africa'.

Formative events during childhood, studies, and marriage

C.F. Beyers Naudé was born during the Rebellion period (1914-15), and he was named after the Boer hero, General C.F. Beyers, for good reason. He grew up in a nationalist and anti-British household, which deeply resented the Anglo-Boer war, and especially the atrocities committed against women and children. His father was a founding member of the Afrikaner Broederbond, strong in the struggle for justice for his own people and also for poor whites in the late 1920s and early 1930s. Beyers Naudé grew up in a household faced by the need for reconciliation with the colonial oppressors of the empire, but also caught up in the bitter battles between nationalists and Smuts's policies of appeasement, as well as the battles within Afrikanerdom for the heart of the "volk" – between the militant Ossewabrandwag and the National Party.[12]

He was touched by a sermon in his father's book on the Rebellion, based on on Gal 3:4, in which the question was asked "whether the Afrikaner people suffered all these things in vain" (see Naudé 1905). His father served as a minister in strongholds of nationalist sentiment, Piet Retief and Graaff Reinet, places where, however, Beyers Naudé, also encountered various Black cultural elements, and also Coloured members trying to attend church in the white Dutch Reformed Church. These childhood experiences opened his mind to the realities of suffering and struggle among people other than his own. These personal experiences began to introduce into his vision another element of reconciliation: with black brothers and sisters who also experienced opp-

---

[12] See for this background Naudé (1995: 35-7); also Pauw (in Hansen 2005: 7-24); Villa-Vicencio (in Villa-Vicencio and De Gruchy: 3-13); and Ryan (1990: 4-11).

ression and marginalisation. The legitimate concern for one's own people's suffering is what later made him recognise the need for Black Consciousness and also the dangers to be avoided in promoting and affirming one's own identity and aspirations at a national level.

It is safe to say that Beyers Naudé's quest for justice was born of his own Afrikaner history, following in the footsteps of his father and General Beyers, whose names he received at baptism during the Rebellion. His quest for reconciliation was likewise the fruit of the same history, with its disagreements and confrontations between Brit and Afrikaner, and between white and black South Africans.

Having grown up in a rather stern household, Beyers Naudé enjoyed the new freedom of self-expression during his study years, 1932-39. At university he excelled in various leadership positions, including Student Representative Council chairperson, chair of the debating society and as Primarius of the prestigious Wilgenhof hostel. It must, however, be said that his theological attention at the "Kweekskool" (the theological seminary at Stellenbosch) was caught by only a handful of people, of whom he always mentioned Professors B.B. Keet and Johannes du Plessis. He would develop his own theology only later, in the praxis of faith in the world, struggling with Biblical texts and truths, which he then realised should have been covered more thoroughly during his theological training.[13]

His mother opposed his marriage to Ilse Weder, born at Genadendal, where her father served in the Moravian mission. His interactions with this missionary context, however, brought him into contact with ecumenical elements and a ministry of inclusion and respect, and his handling of this episode already illustrates the stubborn element in him of following through on his own convictions.[14]

Phases of theological development

The phases of Beyers Naudé's adult life and ministry distinguished here are simply a broad framework within which nuances in his developing thinking about "reconciliation and justice" are placed.[15]

Dutch Reformed Church ministry 1940-63

Given Beyers Naudé's embeddedness in Afrikaner culture, his strong formation through structures of Afrikaner leadership, and his very rapid advance through the ranks to top positions in church and society – also through his Broederbond connections from a very early age – it is not surprising to hear Desmond Tutu speak of him as

---

[13] Naudé 1995: 40-5.
[14] See Pauw in Hansen and Vosloo 2006: 9-10; Pauw in Hansen 2005: 9-10.
[15] I am grateful for the clues given by Coetzee, Hansen and Vosloo (2013) in their introduction and framework to Beyers Naudé's sermon collection. See also the contributions of Christoff Pauw, Margaret Nash and Desmond Tutu in Hansen (2005).

an "unlikely champion of justice".[16] Christoff Pauw, in his short biography, also traces Beyers Naudé's surprising development from "biography of a nationalist" to "shaping an identity of dissent," to "anti-apartheid prophet," and finally to leaving behind "a legacy of justice and reconciliation".[17] In this first period of his ministry in various Dutch Reformed congregations (1940-63), the struggle of moving from "traditional nationalist" to new "identity of dissent" is clearly illustrated. There are already some signs of criticism of the Afrikaner status quo, and a search for a possible alternative route. Here we simply mention, with little elaboration, a few select sermons or events that indicate a certain openness to South African realities, and willingness to work for reconciliation

Wellington 1940-42 and Loxton 1942-45

These were years of war (the Second World War) and of national conflict, for instance the struggles of the militant Ossewabrandwag and the National Party, but also the poor white struggles for survival in the face of the ravages of war and the collapse of the world economy. In his early ministry, Beyers Naudé found himself in difficult *mediating situations* between Afrikaner factions in the congregation, while increasingly realising that poor blacks also needed attention.

From this period, it is interesting to compare two sermons addressing brotherly love in two contexts: vis-à-vis "other groups" in mission work and vis-à-vis intra-Afrikaner politics.[18] In the first one, he speaks openly about stumbling blocks in mission work, showing his understanding of white concerns but, nevertheless, pushing for much more serious engagement by the church in its missionary task. In the second, he calls very directly for reconciliation in a Christian spirit of brotherly love, just before the bitterly contested election of 1943. In the first, he frankly mentioned factors such as liberal mission policies of "equality," doubts about the wisdom of promoting Coloured education and upward mobility, untrustworthiness of the workers, and the high costs of missions – countered by an appeal to God's grace, a vision of the Kingdom of God and a call to Christians to let go of human concerns, while working for and giving generously to the concerns of God's kingdom (Loxton, June 1942). In the other sermon (Loxton 1943), just before the elections in which brother stood against brother (in the bitter battle between the Ossewabrandwag and the National Party), Naudé made a strong appeal for reconciliation and brotherly love. He argues that the real brotherly love of the Bible has to be rediscovered, but also a true biblical sense of justice:

> This is the real point around which everything centres: One cannot expect any unity, love or peace between person and person, group and group, nation and nation if there is no righteousness and justice as a basis for all relations and dealings! Is this not the reason why brotherhood is lacking? Because there are people, groups and nations who feel themselves done in – on social, economic

---

[16] See Tutu in Hansen 2005: 47-54.
[17] See Pauw in Hansen 2005: 7-24.
[18] See Coetzee, Hansen and Vosloo 2013: 51-4 and 63-6.

and political terrain – and thus cannot love? Because misdeeds and injustice block the road which may lead to one another, in home and country! This is for me the big gaping wound, the raw place, the all-determining cause of most of the painful events of our time: a lack of true justice and fairness![19]

Pretoria South 1945-49

Together with his nationalist father, Beyers Naudé supported and joyfully celebrated the National Party victory of 1948 over General Jan Smuts, which was largely based on the underlying Boer-Brit resentment that had not been reconciled. His theological thinking now had to face, and include, *justice and reconciliation issues*, including the harsh reality of intra-Afrikaner strife or *"broedertwis"*.

Just before the crucial 1948 elections, Beyers Naudé again called (at Olifantsfontein, 23 May 1948), for responsible participation by all Christians, avoiding the slogan that "politics is dirty." No, he said, politics is exactly the area in which Christian convictions should act as "salt," where Christians should ask which policies will give God the glory, which candidates will show courage to do the right thing, to serve God's truth?[20] Interestingly, shortly before that, on 25 January 1948, he addressed racial friction in a sermon on Matthew 10:16: "Therefore be as shrewd as snakes and innocent as doves".[21] He claims the country is reaping the fruits of selfish policies (e.g., creating cheap labour by importing Indian workers, which led to racial friction with black workers, who felt hard done by); also the fruits of a lack of evangelical zeal to energetically bring the gospel to blacks and Indians alike. He also blames the whites for leading by the example of violence (arms) to deal with conflict and points out that injustices by whichever group vis-à-vis another cannot be hidden in history, but will always eventually be revealed and come to light.

Pretoria East 1949-55 and Potchefstroom 1955-59

As a minister to students in both these congregations, he met young critical theologians such as David Bosch and Ben Marais,[22] and felt himself challenged by Keet's early, and at the time rather forceful, critique of apartheid (Keet 1956). He was also deeply influenced by an extensive study tour to investigate Christian youth work in postwar Europe. This experience triggered in him a new vision for ministry in South Africa, involving much more than concern for his own people, as legitimate as that might be. Apartheid needed to be confronted theologically with *a theology of justice on the basis of real reconciliation*.

---

[19] Coetzee, Hansen and Vosloo 2013: 65
[20] Coetzee, Hansen and Vosloo 2013: 95-6.
[21] Coetzee, Hansen and Vosloo 2013: 93-4.
[22] He was deeply influenced by Marais (1952).

His sermons from this period are clearly aimed at building up positive faith perspectives for Christian living amid societal issues:[23] about joyful living in all circumstances, true compassion, dedication, communion of the holy, mission problems to be overcome, true worship and the spirit of Christmas. However, regularly there is also a critical tone, and questions are raised in a pastoral spirit. Such a sermon, dealing with the half-built tower of Luke 14:28-13, was preached on 1 August 1954. One of its questions was whether the Dutch Reformed Church had the courage to either complete its work fully of creating a just segregated society, or if that task showed itself to be unviable, to ask the painful but logical questions honestly:

> Suppose this ideal is no longer practically implementable, if it is clearly too late to complete the task? What is then the alternative which we as church and as Christians can present? Are we prepared to look this alternative squarely in the eye, to drop our plan in view of God's gospel, and to ask: Is this a viable conviction, or is it only half-baked? If we as Christians will not study this and think it through carefully, who will do it? [24]

Aasvoëlkop 1959-63

As is well-known, Naudé's years in the elite congregation of Aasvoëlkop, at a time when he was poised for glory in the Afrikaner establishment, coincided with two earth-shaking events: Sharpeville (where the police, in panic, shot 69 people protesting relatively peacefully), and Cottesloe (the ecumenical consultation on apartheid at which a number of leading Dutch Reformed ministers, including Naudé, strongly opposed apartheid and the injustices accompanying its implementation). These events made it impossible for him to not take a decisive stand, with decisive consequences, especially when he and his colleagues were rudely repudiated, first by the prime minister, Dr H.F. Verwoerd, and then by various Dutch Reformed Church synods. Sharpeville and Cottesloe finally brought about Beyers Naudé's firm and resolute stand against apartheid, with an accompanying theology and praxis that combined justice and reconciliation.

This new prophetic urgency is clearly evident in the texts of all the sermons from this time that have been taken up in Coetzee, Hansen and Vosloo.[25] Here I deal only cryptically with a few of them.

In a sermon on the Day of the Covenant (16 December 1959), he concludes that what is needed from white Christians in South Africa in view of God's guidance in their history is total dedication to God's work, much greater eagerness for mission and a willingness to make sacrifices in the cause of God's kingdom. This also involved

---

[23] Coetzee, Hansen and Vosloo 2013: 103-38.
[24] Coetzee, Hansen and Vosloo 2013: 108. Here he was in fact directly questioning the conclusions reached by G.D. Scholtz in his influential book, *Het die Afrikanervolk 'n toekoms?* ("Do the Afrikaner people have a future?"). Scholtz answered by stating that they would only be secure through the consistent application of apartheid in all areas of life.
[25] Coetzee, Hansen and Vosloo 2013: 139-76.

taking responsibility for the well-being of people working for or with them, their education to live up to their full potential, and showing non-white brothers and sisters the self-sacrificing love of Christ. Finally, white Christians needed to commit to serious dialogue in which the agenda was not only the self-preservation of Afrikaners, but also harmonious coexistence between white and black. [26]

On 10 April 1960, just after Sharpeville and a day after the attempt on Prime Minister Verwoerd's life, Naudé preached on Isaiah 54:14: "In righteousness you will be established".[27] He calmly makes a case that the way into the future, the way of survival for all the warring factions in South Africa can only be the way of God's justice, as shown by Jesus (along the lines of the suffering Servant, who opposed all injustice by being willing to suffer personally for the achievement of justice and salvation for all of us, as described in the previous chapter of Isaiah).

> If we want to ask what justice is, we should ask what Jesus asks from us through his Word, attitude and deed – that is the highest form of righteousness! Not justice in the form of laws and rules, or power and violence, or anger and revenge, NO. For the Christian the big question remains: What justice does Jesus require from me to do, to my own people and race, just as to other people and races?

Two other – much-quoted – sermons from this period, when Beyers Naudé was struggling with himself and with his congregation to gain clarity on the way forward, include the one he preached at Auckland Park on 22 September 1963 on Acts 5:29, when he announced his acceptance of editorship of *Pro Veritate* ("We must obey God rather than men"),[28] and his farewell sermon at Aasvoëlkop on 3 November 1963, on the words of Jeremiah 23:29 ("Is not my word like fire and like a hammer that breaks a rock in pieces?").[29]

---

[26] Coetzee, Hansen and Vosloo 2013: 140-1.
[27] Coetzee, Hansen and Vosloo 2013: 151.
[28] Coetzee, Hansen and Vosloo 2013: 163-7. In November 1960 he preached a sermon on the same text at Linden, and again in December 1960 at Piet Retief, showing that since Sharpeville he had really been grappling with the issue of obedience to God's call. On 27 May 1962, he frankly addressed the critical question of what his whole ministry was about in his prophetic protest against apartheid (which by that time had become quite controversial and a topic of much debate). This question he addressed in a strong sermon on 1 Corinthians 2:2: "For I resolved to know nothing while I was with you except Jesus Christ and him crucified" (Coetzee, Hansen and Vosloo 2013: 159-62). All that he said later about reconciliation and justice has to be understood within this framework of obediently, and truthfully, following Christ – the suffering servant of God's purposes.
[29] Coetzee, Hansen and Vosloo 2013: 169-73. The final paragraph of this sermon reads as follows: "The answer to all our questions, the light on our way ahead, the hope for our future, lies in full obedience to him as Living Word – and in Him alone. The answer, the light, the hope, lies in full obedience to Him as Living Word – and in Him alone!" (Coetzee, Hansen and Vosloo 2013: 173).

A white-only residential area near Cape Town 1970.

Assertive ecumenical orientation and action 1963-73

The year 1963 thus signalled the fact that Beyers Naudé inevitably was confronted with a radical choice: to continue with his Dutch Reformed Church ministry in a more critical fashion, by including ecumenical perspectives, relevant Bible Studies, and prophetic preaching, or by breaking away to launch Pro Veritate as a vehicle of wider critical thinking and communication. He chose the latter, for ecumenical engagement and *"oop gesprek"* (open dialogue), convinced that people could be persuaded over time to change their thinking and attitudes to create an open, unified and reconciling church.

Here interesting questions arise: Was this a precursor of Habermas's idea of "communicative action"? The two men were definitely thinking along the same lines! Was he anticipating Belhar? He was clearly an early proponent of the critical theology out of which the Belhar Confession emerged!

Through these last sermons at Aasvoëlkop, he wished to convey a crystal clear message: the road he was called upon, away from the Dutch Reformed ministry into the search for truth (Pro Veritate) and into a new Christian commitment for justice (the Christian Institute) was a way of obedience, of utter commitment to Jesus Christ, whose own life was poured into the service of righteousness for others. And the key text of his sermon on 15 December 1963, when taking over the leadership of the CI, shows with equal clarity that this new ministry was a *ministry of reconciliation – in justice*.

Over the next 10 years, Beyers Naudé's life was poured into ecumenical work – building strong networks across many boundaries, in Africa, Europe and the US. His attendance at the ground-breaking World Council of Churches meeting in 1966 in Geneva on "Church and Society" inspired him and others in the South African struggle to move from a confessional church to a *confessing* church, with emphasis on *reconciliation praxis*. This new focus was also given impetus by *The Message to the People* (produced ecumenically in September 1968).[30]

A few key sentences illustrate the central role of Christian reconciliation in this message of hope to the oppressed people of South Africa:

> The Gospel of Jesus Christ is the good news that in Christ God has broken down the walls of division between God and man, and between man and man ... The Gospel of Jesus Christ declares that God is reconciling us to himself and to each other; and that therefore such barriers as race and nationality have no rightful place in the inclusive brotherhood of Christian disciples ... We believe that this doctrine of separation is a false faith, a novel gospel; it inevitably is in conflict with the Gospel of Jesus Christ, which offers salvation, both individual and social, through faith in Christ alone ... A policy of separation is a demonstration of unbelief in the power of the Gospel; any demonstration of the reality of reconciliation would endanger this policy ... And so, we wish to put to every Christian person in the country the question which we ourselves face each day; to whom, or to what, are you giving your first loyalty, your primary commitment? Is it to a subsection of mankind, an ethnic group, a human tradition, a political idea, or to Christ?

Another major initiative along the same theological lines was launched by the CI, jointly with the SACC, in mid-1969: SPROCAS, or the Study Project on Christianity in Apartheid Society. This project, including six commissions and a diverse set of over 140 commissioners and consultants, focused on the need for change in South Africa in all areas – economics, education, law, politics and the church. The initial phase of this project, SPROCAS I, aimed at convincing whites to realise what was going on and change their hearts and ways towards reconciliation and justice. It was followed by SPROCAS 2, which was much more focused on black empowerment against apartheid – thus leading to a strong focus on Black Consciousness. To combine these two elements, Beyers Naudé believed that a strong theology of real reconciliation was needed.

The "Lean Years" 1973-84

It was at just about the time that the National Party started to clamp down on so-called "affected organisations," in the case of the CI principally through the Schlebusch Commission, that Beyers Naudé and the CI reached out to the African Independent Churches Association, helping these churches with literature and basic theological training. Perhaps even more important, this was also the time when the CI gave strong support

---

[30] See the authorised summary in Naudé 1995: 167-9.

The young boy Hector Pieterson was one of many protestors and bystanders killed by fierce police brutality in the Soweto Uprising on 16 June 1976. The iconic photo of the 18-year-old school boy Mbuyisa Makhubo carrying him in his arms, and his sister, Antoinette Sithole, running beside them, is displayed at the Hector Pieterson Memorial in Soweto.

to Steve Biko's ideas on Black Consciousness.[31] This support acknowledged that blacks had the right to stand up to oppressors, just as the Afrikaner people had done to the British Empire. It also acknowledged that they had to develop a strong consciousness of their own worth, but also of their own complicity in their oppression, which would persist if they did not clearly address the justice issues involved. They also needed to heed the lessons of the Afrikaner struggle and not become separated from other people' struggles and pain. Their struggle for justice needed to fit into a much bigger, comprehensive notion of reconciliation.

A key document in this phase is on "Divine or Civil Disobedience," 24 September 1973, a submission against the skewed workings of the Schlebusch Commission. It was not enough, however, to prevent the CI from being declared an "affected organisation" on 30 May 1975.[32] This eventually led to the banning of the CI and house arrest for Beyers Naudé (for the "seven lean years," 1977-84), but could not prevent the trig-

---

[31] Beyers Naudé's biggest breakthrough as a white Christian, theologian and activist, according to his later reflections in his autobiography, was the realisation that the reality of the black experience had to be approached through the legitimate and authentic experiences and expressions of black Christians and black people themselves. All future ecumenical work would have to reopen these pages of history to include and integrate African independent church theology and Black Consciousness in whatever new forms it might again manifest itself authentically (see Naudé 1995: 83-96). Reconciliation and justice cannot be approached via "white definitions" only: they are human realities that need to reflect all human experiences of God's justice and God's love, of good and bad, right and wrong.

[32] It is interesting that Naudé (1995: 100-2) stresses that churches would do well in the current post-apartheid situation to revisit this document, to understand the deep levels of mistrust and manipulation that were at work in the ideology of apartheid and to understand the challenging agenda of reconciliation.

gering of a deeper level of theological protest via Black Consciousness and eventually also Liberation Theology. A key issue became resistance to unjust rule and oppression, thus linking the struggle against racism with the struggle against oppression in terms of economic dominance and "class." In this context, various events played a crucial role in sharpening Beyers Naudé's understanding of reconciliation, which for him could never be a cheap concept, unrelated to God's justice and restoration of human dignity. A key event in this regard was the 1974 Hammanskraal meeting at which the SACC decided to campaign against military conscription. This was soon followed by the Soweto youth uprising of 1976 – most probably the watershed event in the intensifying struggle against oppression and apartheid, leading to general uprisings against the government everywhere, seemingly uncontrollably. Part of the resentment and anger that fuelled these strong protests was the banning of various organisations, including the CI, which was finally shut down by the apartheid government on 19 October 1977. Beyers Naudé himself was also immediately placed under house arrest for five years (which eventually became seven years!).

A text that fits in here, again reflecting the central role of reconciliation in the work of the CI and again dealing with 2 Cor 5:6-9 and the need for both deep reconciliation and justice is "A valid Christian ministry," a sermon delivered at Yeoville Anglican Church on 22 February 1976.[33] Here Naudé confirms the "validity" of the central Christian task of the church, reconciliation, "entrusted to it by Christ." He said: "Reconciliation in biblical terms can only be achieved on the basis of justice otherwise it will be meaningless; no reconciliation can therefore be possible unless it is achieved on the basis of solidarity with the oppressed".[34]

Similar points on reconciliation were raised even more pointedly in his address to graduates of the Federal Theological Seminary in Edendale, Pietermaritzburg on 16 March 1977, not long before his house arrest, on the topic of "Christian ministry in a time of crisis".[35] In formulations such as the following, one can sense in no uncertain terms the urgency of the crisis facing the ministry of reconciliation:

I am aware that many blacks, including black Christians, have become increasingly suspicious when whites approach them with the plea for reconciliation. They state unequivocally: you whites want reconciliation while we blacks seek liberation, and only when you are prepared to identify yourself with our goal for liberation can there be true reconciliation. Without that, any such plea could never be realised.[36]

Through various contributions, many in the form of wonderful anecdotes, to Coetzee, Muller and Hansen (2015), the ironical truth of his "years of captivity" has become more and more apparent.[37] The "lean years" of isolation and house arrest became years

---

[33] Coetzee, Hansen and Vosloo 2013: 185-7.

[34] Coetzee, Hansen and Vosloo 2013: 186.

[35] Coetzee, Hansen and Vosloo 2006: 81-9.

[36] Hansen and Vosloo 2006:88.

[37] See, for instance, the contributions of John de Gruchy, Horst Kleinschmidt, Rudolph Meyer and others in the section on the CI (pp. 3-92); Albert Nolan, Desmond Tutu and others in the section on ecumenical contacts (pp. 211-90), and the section on overseas contacts

Beyers Naudé in Johannesburg 1981

in which the seeds of hope were sown far and wide via individual conversations by hundreds of Christians from South Africa, and all over the world, with Beyers Naudé. In these conversations, for which he had all the time in the world and engaged in with total dedication, the depth of Christian commitment that would be needed for true liberation and true reconciliation can be fathomed over and over again. With what divine irony can we now look back on the fact that exactly when the struggle was at its peak, at its most intense, in the mid-1980s, Beyers Naudé was released from his isolation, became general secretary of the SACC, and could be part of the new phase, the end phase, of the struggle!

Kairos, Belhar and Liberation (1985-95)

The final phases of the breakthrough to justice and liberation in South Africa, the agenda for which Beyers Naudé and his family sacrificed so much, is well documented, and we cannot deal with the details here. Suffice it to summarise a number of crucial initiatives. Beyers Naudé, fully "back in business" as general secretary of the SACC (from February 1985 till July 1988), and following in the footsteps of the very recent Nobel Peace Laureate and newly appointed Bishop of Johannesburg, Desmond Tutu, again had a very strong hand, upfront or behind the scenes, in most of these initiatives.

Among the crucial initiatives in this particularly hard phase of the struggle were the Broederkring, later called the *Belydende Kring* (Confessional Circle) that was formed in the Dutch Reformed Mission Church, with Allan Boesak as a leading figure, and in the Dutch Reformed Church. There was also the so-called "Open Letter" by an influential group of theologians and ministers – initiatives towards reconciliation in justice, strongly supported and encouraged by Beyers Naudé. During his term as SACC general secretary two major confessional documents were born, the Kairos Document of 1985-86, driven by the Institute for Contextual Theology, with Father Albert Nolan as a leading force, and the Belhar Confession (of 1982/1986), a new Reformed Confession on the unity, reconciliation and justice tasks of the church. It is fair to argue and easy to illustrate that these two documents together capture the spirit of Beyers Naudé's "theology of reconciliation" by walking on the two legs he had emphasised all along: justice and reconciliation. There could be no reconciliation without justice, no justice

---

(pp.291-314). See Naudé (1995: 113-23) for his own humble, and far too brief, account of these years. From Horst Kleinschmidt's account, the "lean years" were not just spent in one-on-one consultations, influential as these may have been, but also in a flurry of clandestine, underground activities involving links with the Programme to Combat Racism at the World Council of Churches, Kairos in the Netherlands, various donor organisations and banned organisations in South Africa (including the ANC).

without the spirit and reality of reconciliation! [38]

The further clamp-down by the desperate apartheid government, by means of ever more repressive state of emergency measures, only led to the determined formation of the United Democratic Front. This was followed by the emergence of the broadly based United Democratic Movement, strongly supported by various religious groups and civil society at large, and led by charismatic figures such as Desmond Tutu, Allan Boesak and Beyers Naudé – together with a host of civil society leaders – marching as it were "at the front."

Vindication

All these prophetic and courageous activities of a confessional church, even a confessional movement, vindicated the belief of leaders such as Beyers Naudé and Desmond Tutu that we live in a moral universe, that there is no future without forgiveness and reconciliation, just as there is no future and no peace without justice. The events of the late 1980s, when the forces of radical resistance could have caused total chaos. However, this was avertedby the take-over by de Klerk from Botha, the unbanning of the ANC and various other organisations, the peace talks, elections, the writing of the new constitution and eventually the Truth and Reconciliation Commission headed by Archbishop Desmond Tutu – all these taken together were a vindication of Beyers Naudé's lifelong struggle to combine a theology of justice and protest with a theology of reconciliation and peace.

The final text, in many ways, then is – as one might expect – the sermon on "Reconciliation" delivered by Beyers Naudé to his own people at his beloved Aasvoëlkop on 13 August 1995: [39]

> If I have to capture the key events of this period in two words, I cannot find better ones than *confrontation* and *reconciliation*. This was an extended period of bitter confrontation and conflict about which we need not talk today, but if anyone is reading the signs of the times correctly now, then the new period we enter will be one of reconciliation ... on all levels of society: political, religiously, culturally, educationally, economic.

He then stresses that Paul discovered the deep secrets of God's reconciliation, which have serious consequences for the world and for all of us:

> God did not only reconcile a handful of believers, or exclusively the church as the body of Christ, but the *world*, thus the whole human communion. What a massive truth with far-reaching consequences for the Church and the Kingdom of God! No wonder that Paul, deep under the impression of this truth,

---

[38] Elaborating the details of such an interpretation of Naudé in relation to Kairos and Belhar will have to be the work of another day.

[39] Naudé 1995: 189-92.

proclaims: "We beg you on behalf of Christ: accept the reconciliation with God which He has worked out!"… Is this possible at all? The person belonging to Christ is a new creature, a new human being, the old has passed. God has given us the ministry of reconciliation.

And then, typically, he proceeds to mention a whole handful of "tasks" that await us… We can only honour this great son of South Africa by tackling these tasks, in the direction of "justice for all" and in the spirit of reconciliation.

References

V. Brümmer (2013), *Vroom of Regsinnig? Teologie in die NG Kerk*. Stellenbosch: Bybel-Media.

M. Coetzee, L. Hansen and R. Vosloo (eds.) (2013), *Vreesloos gehoorsaam. 'n Keur uit Beyers Naudé se preke 1939-1997*. Stellenbosch: Sun Press

M. Coetzee, R. Muller and L. Hansen (eds.) (2015), *Cultivating seeds of hope. Conversations on the life of Beyers Naudé*. Stellenbosch: Sun Press

L. Hansen (ed.) (2005), *The legacy of Beyers Naudé*. Stellenbosch: Sun Press

L. Hansen and R. Vosloo (eds.) (2006), *Oom Bey for the future. Engaging the witness of Beyers Naudé*. Stellenbosch: Sun Press

B.B. Keet (1956), *Whither South Africa?* Stellenbosch: University Publishers and Booksellers

B. Marais (1952), *Die kleur krisis in die Weste*. Johannesburg, Goeie Hoop Uitgewers (*Colour: unsolved problem of the West*. Cape Town: Howard B. Timmins)

B. Naudé (1995), *My land van hoop. Die lewe van Beyers Naudé*. Johannesburg/Cape Town/Pretoria: Human & Rousseau

J.F. Naudé (1905), *Vechten en vluchten van Beyers en Kemp*. Rotterdam: Nijgh & Van Ditmar

C. Ryan (1990), *Beyers Naudé. Pilgrimage of faith*. Claremont, Cape Town: David Philip

C. Villa-Vicencio and J.W. De Gruchy (eds.) (1985), *Resistance and Hope. South African essays in honour of Beyers Naudé*. Cape Town: David Philip

Johannesburg, 19 September 1990. Meeting about the Swedish-South African ecumenical scholarship exchange program at the Ecumenical Advice Bureau. In the photo to the left we see, from left: Rune Forsbeck, Tom Nkoana, Omon Norén, Keith Bingle and Beyers Naudé.

A Response to Christo Lombard

Rune Forsbeck

My remarks are to be understood more as questions than as declarations. I am no scholar, but a pastor. From August 1985 until 1994, I served as general secretary of the Swedish Ecumenical Council. So first Beyers and I were colleagues – as he in 1985 was general secretary of the South African Council of Churches. After his retirement, we cooperated within the framework of his Ecumenical Advice Bureau (EAB). I applied in the name of my council for money from the Swedish government and channelled large sums to a scholarship programme run by Beyers and the EAB. So I got to know Beyers more in terms of practical and administrative work than in sharing theological thoughts and deliberations. Therefore, not so many declarations on my part, but questions to you who knew him better as a theologian.

Obedience to God

Christo's thesis is, as we heard, that Beyers's ministry was based on *obedience to God* (and I think that it is important to stress obedience *to God*, not just obedience) and *reconciliation*. If anything should be added to that I would propose the *Word of God* (as we find it in the Bible), *ecumenism* and *evangelisation*. In his letter of resignation to the Broederbond, he wrote, among other things:

> I want to mention the refusal to allow non whites to attend services in our Church, the fear of making *closer religious contact* with these people and the irreparable harm it inflicts on our efforts to *Christianise the heathen*. – These objections do not arise in me from political considerations or out of personal

interest, even less from a false liberalism or worldly humanism. They are the fruit of my Christian convictions and my *observations of the Bible* (Ryan 1990: 92).

As a parenthesis: For us in Sweden – and especially for us who belonged to the Mission Covenant Church of Sweden, now a part of the Uniting Church in Sweden – it is interesting that Christo chose a sermon by Beyers on verses 15 to 21 in the fifth chapter of St Paul's second letter to the Corinthians. This very text played a basic role in the theological debate – not to say fight – that took place in our country at the end of the 19th century. The main figure in that struggle was Paul Petter Waldenström, by many considered to be the founder of the Mission Covenant Church of Sweden.

Reconcilium

The word *reconciliation* stems from the Latin *concilium*, meaning "gathering," "meeting," "conference," "assembly" and the like. The prefix *co-*, or *com-*, or *con-* stands for "together," "with" and so forth. The element *cilium* is derived from the word *calare*, meaning "call out." That means that somebody has had to take the initiative in calling a meeting, otherwise a meeting would not take place. And the same applies to the term reconciliation, as re means "again," "once more". To reconcile is to "restore the concilium", to create and form an organ for deliberation.

When Beyers Naudé served as pastor in various congregations, the divine service was very important to him. I think that was because he saw worship as a tool for reconciliation, not only between God and man but also between different groups of people. Worship is – or should be – a "*reconcilium*".

Deeply spiritual and profoundly secular

In her book *Beyers Naudé: Pilgrimage of Faith*, Colleen Ryan cites Charles Villa-Vicencio in his and J.W. de Gruchy's *Resistance and Hope: South African Essays in Honour of Beyers Naudé*, published in 1985. Villa Vicencio says:

> Today, when he [Beyers Naudé] is asked to explain theologically what the Word of God is, his response is rather precise. "It is … one's understanding of the declared will of God made known in the Scriptures." This must be tested within in a community of people of goodwill, including both Christians and those who care not to be known as such. It must be concretised in relation to ongoing political and economic analysis, and ultimately verified in a deeply personal inner conviction. He is today at once a deeply spiritual and a profoundly secular person. (Ryan 1990: 45)

First and foremost a minister

Christo says about Beyers's study years that he "would develop his own theology later in praxis of faith in the world." And Colleen Ryan starts one of her sentences in her book thus: "Although not considered a 'great theologian'…" (Ryan 1990: 53).

I think that is true. I may be wrong, but I think that he was not a "great theologian" from an academic point of view. He was first and foremost a minister, pastor, a servant of the Word of God, a preacher. He didn't just *think* theology. Theology for him was not only a theoretical matter. It was the basis and starting point for *action*. He *created* theology by living in obedience to the word of God. I don't know, but I guess that the words of Jesus in John 3:21 were very important to him. There Jesus says, in Greek: χω δε ποιόν την αλήθειαν ερχεται προς το φως. In the *New International Version of the Holy Bible* it is translated as: "But whoever lives by the truth comes into the light" and in *The New English Bible* as: "The honest man comes to the light," but a literal translation would be "But he who does the truth comes to the light," and that is the way in which King James Version renders the sentence. There we read: "But he that doeth truth cometh to the light." As a matter of fact, the well reputed French translation, *Traduction oecuménique de la Bible*, has the same: "Celui qui fait la vérité vient a la lumière." In any case, the theology of reconciliation, in the spirit of Beyers Naudé, is not first of all – or just – a theory, a system of principles, but a way of living, a manner of life.

The man in the photo

In June 1985, the German theologian Dorothee Sölle and Beyers Naudé met in the Netherlands for a conversation. The interviewer showed Dr Sölle a picture. It was the photo, well-known to us, of Beyers with his parents and brother Joos, photographed shortly after the brother's ordination in 1940. Dorothee Sölle asked: "What happened to the man in this photo?" And Beyers answered:

> I think there are three major factors which contributed to my conversion. The first is a theological one … I knew the stand which my church had taken with regard to apartheid. And that led me to a self study of the traditional ways in which the Dutch Reformed Church justified the whole policy of apartheid on biblical grounds. I did this study in between, and eventually came to the conclusion that there was no way in which I could justify on biblical grounds the whole policy of apartheid, as was done by my church. There was no way I could subscribe to the interpretation which they gave to certain passages of the Old and the New Testament. These were either unconsciously or deliberately so distorted, so one sided, so politically or ideologically motivated and loaded, that for the first time, you know, there was this theological crisis in my life (Naudé and Sölle).

The basis for Beyers Naudé as a theologian was the Bible, the Word of God, and the obedience to the truth he found revealed there. After a while, Beyers continues:

> I think of a second event in my life, or a series of events, which subsequently I saw to be, if I may describe it in this way, the hand of God guiding me into a new direction. It was the fact that I was elected as acting moderator of the Transvaal Synod, and in that position, young ministers – white ministers – who were serving African and coloured and Indian congregations came to me with the problems which they were experiencing within their own congregations, the painful experiences of their own people with what apartheid laws were doing to them. And when they came to me and described what they themselves had experienced, I could not believe it. I knew them well, because they were students when I was a university pastor in Pretoria. There was a very fine, open, warm relationship between us and I said to them: "It's impossible, it can't be." And then they invited me to go to their congregations, which I did. I met with their church councils, I met with members of the congregation, I met with families who were deeply divided because, for instance, of the mixed marriages act, and the group areas act, and I was shattered. It was an experience which led me to the situation of being totally lost.

And then Beyers mentions the third event:

> Then came Sharpeville … On 21 March 1960, a peaceful protest march of people was disrupted by 69 people being shot, most of them in their back when they fled, and that in a certain sense culminated the whole situation. And there was no way in which I could get out of it any longer. (Naudé and Sölle 1986: 4-5)

Reconciliation and ecumenism

As mentioned at the beginning, I met Beyers for the first time when I was new as general secretary of the Swedish Ecumenical Council – and Beyers held the same position in the South African Council of Churches. Already in creating and working for the Christian Institute his deep *ecumenical* conviction had been obvious and found expression. And I think that there is a very close connection between *reconciliation* and *ecumenism*. The fundamental idea behind reconciliation and the efforts to reconcile must be that all mankind – humanity – is *one* and that it is possible to reunite what has been torn apart. And the fundamental idea behind ecumenism is exactly the same: The church is *one*, and it is a scandal that it is divided and pulled asunder by different groups. As God has created only *one* world, he has intended only *one* church, and the church is called to be united not for its own sake only, but for the reconciliation and unity of the whole world, the whole of mankind. If you are guided by such a conviction you have to draw political conclusions from it. I think that was what Beyers did.

In his conversation with Dorothee Sölle, Beyers said:

> We have also misunderstood the concept of reconciliation so that the church, or many parts of the church leadership, believe that you can only be a reconciling agent if you are neutral, and that's not possible (Naudé and Sölle 1986: 27).

But if a pastor has to draw political conclusions from his interpretation of the Gospel, and if he or she cannot be neutral, in what way is he or she to express his/her political engagement? My personal answer is that you – as a pastor – should not be or act as a politician but that you should encourage those in your congregation who are appropriate for political work to commit themselves to it. And my question: Would you say that Beyers acted in this way?

In the process that led to Beyers's leaving the Broederbond, Albert Geyser wrote in 1963 about the Broederbond documents he had read: "What I read in these documents convinced me in an increasing measure that they were aimed at making use of the Church for political aims." He argued that the Broederbond was "making the Church, which is the Bride of Christ, a handmaiden of politics" (Ryan 1990: 93). As we talk about "Faith as politics," maybe we should take his words as a danger signal.

Christo has used some of Beyers's sermons to illustrate how his ministry for justice in South Africa was carried, all along, by his deep sense that reconciliation was at the heart of the gospel. I think this is the right way. Beyers was convinced that principles for a good human and divine life were revealed to us in the Bible. Rightly understood and interpreted, the Bible, to him, was the Word of God. All through his life he placed immense importance on Bible study, and he was above all, as I understand it, a Bible teacher and preacher. In the Bible, he saw principles, guidelines and values fundamental not only to a righteous life at an individual level, but for the life and ethos of a whole community, a society, a nation. Of course it is interesting to ponder the question of to what extent his background as a *boer* – as a member of a *volk* – influenced him in this respect, but I think it more appropriate – with regard to our theme, "Faith as Politics" – to ask the question if, and to what extent the pastor, the preacher – and also the spiritual guide – should be a politician.

I have a thought that probably has nothing, or at least very little, to do with our topic "Faith as Politics." But I ask myself if Jesus' words in Matthew 19:5 about marriage and divorce are applicable also to other relations among people. Are these (also) words against apartheid when he says: "Therefore what God has joined together, let man not separate"?

References

C.F. Beyers Naudé and Dorothee Sölle (1986), *Hope for Faith – a conversation*. Grand Rapids: WCC Publications, Eerdmans

C. Ryan (1990), *Beyers Naudé: Pilgrimage of faith*. Cape Town: David Philip

C. Villa-Vicencio and J.W. De Gruchy (eds.) (1985), *Resistance and Hope: South African essays in honour of Beyers Naudé*. Cape Town: David Philip

The Holy Bible (n.d.) King James Version. Cleveland and New York: World Publishing Company

The Holy Bible (1979), New International Version. London: Hodder and Stoughton

The New English Bible (1961), New Testament. Oxford and Cambridge: Oxford University Press and Cambridge University Press

Traduction Oecuménique de la Bible (1971-82), Paris: Alliance Biblique Universelle

Rune Forsbeck, born in 1938, obtained his BD in Uppsala in 1965 and was ordained a pastor in the Swedish Mission Covenant Church in 1966. He has served as a congregational pastor in Uppsala and Lidingö and as University Chaplain in Uppsala (1970-75). Between 1985 and 1993, he was the General Secretary of the Swedish Ecumenical Council, and from 1994 until his retirement in 2004 as a Health Care Chaplaincy Consultant. He lives in Lidingö.

Birgitta Karlström-Dorph, born in 1939, is a Swedish ambassador who served in Africa for 20 years. She was the deputy head of mission in South Africa from 1982 until 1988.

Ben Khumalo-Seegelken, theologian, and social scientist, was born in 1950 and worked at the Edendale Lay Ecumenical Centre near Pietermaritzburg, South Africa (1972-75), promoting political awareness through youth programmes in and around Pietermaritzburg and Durban. In 1975, he had to leave the country as a political refugee and gained asylum in West Germany. He is a critical observer of the political and social situation in and around South Africa and serves in various networks in Germany and in South Africa, including the Beyers Naudé Centre for Public Theology at the University of Stellenbosch and the Khulumani Support Group in Johannesburg. He regular posts South Africa-related news and analyses on his web site: www.benkhumalo-seegelken.de.

Horst Kleinschmidt, born in 1945, worked at the Christian Institute (CI) from 1972. He was part of the team that translated the Study Project on Christianity in Apartheid Society (SPROCAS) recommendations into action projects. With Peter Randall, he ran the White Community Programme (later changed to the Programme for Social Change). In 1975, he was appointed assistant to Beyers Naudé but was detained under the notorious Terrorism Act a few weeks later. After 73 days in solitary confinement, he was released without charge or court proceedings. Six months later, when rumours of his re-detention reached him, he was flown "as a parcel" in the back of a small aircraft by CI colleague Cedric Mayson to safety in Botswana. Eventually, he was given asylum in the Netherlands, where he served as external representative of the CI until October 1979, when the apartheid government outlawed the CI and banned (house arrested) its leading staff members. First from the Netherlands and later from his exile domicile in London, he built an underground network with his colleagues back home. He returned to South Africa in 1992 after he was granted indemnity from political prosecution. Now retired, he writes about the history he lived through, as well as the history of his family during the colonial and apartheid periods in both South Africa and Namibia. Find out more at his website: www.horstkleinschmidt.co.za.

Christo Lombard, born in 1948, was raised in Windhoek. He is the Desmond Tutu Chair for Ecumenical Theology and Social Transformation, and Acting Director of the

Desmond Tutu Centre for Spirituality and Society, at the University of Western Cape. Previously he was Chair of the Department of Religion and Theology at the University of Namibia and Director of the Ecumenical Institute for Namibia. During the struggle for the liberation in Namibia, he was active in the founding of the Namibia Peace Plan 435 Study and Contact Group (Deputy Chairperson 1986-89) and after independence in the Breaking the Wall of Silence Movement (Secretary, 1996-2002). As an active member of Namibian civil society, he was also Chairperson (1996-2000) of the Project for the Study of Violence and Reconciliation in Namibia (now: The PEACE Centre), and a board member of the Forum for the Future.

Henning Melber, born in 1950, came to Namibia as a son of German immigrants in 1967. He studied Political Science and Sociology at the Freie Universität Berlin and obtained his PhD in Political Science in 1980 and his Habilitation (venia legend in Development Studies) in 1993 at the University of Bremen. He joined SWAPO in 1974 and from 1975 was banned from entering Namibia (until 1989) and South Africa (until 1993). He was Senior Lecturer in International Politics at the University of Kassel (1982-92), Director of the Namibian Economic Policy Research Unit (NEPRU) in Windhoek (1992-2000), Research Director at the Nordic Africa Institute (2000-06) and Executive Director at the Dag Hammarskjöld Foundation (2006-12) and remains a Senior Advisor to both institutions in Uppsala. He is Extraordinary Professor at the Department of Political Science, University of Pretoria and the Centre for Africa Studies, University of the Free State in Bloemfontein and a Senior Research Fellow at the Institute for Commonwealth Studies/School for Advanced Study at the University of London.

Barney Pityana, born in 1945, is retired Vice Chancellor of the University of South Africa (Unisa). He was trained in law in South Africa and admitted as an attorney of the High Court of South Africa, read Theology in London and trained for the Anglican ministry at Ripon College Cuddesdon, Oxford. As ordained priest in the Church of England, he served in parishes in England and was Director of the World Council of Churches' Programme to Combat Racism. He obtained a PhD in Religious Studies from the University of Cape Town and served later as the inaugural Chairperson of the South African Human Rights Commission, and as a member of the African Commission on Human and Peoples' Rights. He is Professor emeritus in Law at Unisa and Honorary Professor at the Allan Gray Centre for Leadership Ethics at the Department of Philosophy, Rhodes University in Grahamstown. He has received honorary degrees from Argentina, Canada and the United States and is also Fellow of King's College London, Ripon College Cuddesdon and the Commonwealth of Learning. He is a member of the Academy of Science of South Africa (ASSAf) and General Secretary of the Network of African Academies of Science.

www.ingramcontent.com/pod-product-compliance
Lightning Source LLC
Chambersburg PA
CBHW081507040426
42446CB00017B/3430